Preaching on the Common Worship Lectionary

The author is currently preaching in over forty churches, three and often four times each Sunday, and occasionally also during the week, mainly in the Diocese of Derby.

Licensed in 1986, she was shortlisted in 1997 for *The Times*/College of Preachers' 'Preacher of the Year', with her sermon on Luke 14.34–35 being published in *The Times Best Sermons of 1998* (Cassell, 1998); and again in 1999, with her sermon on this occasion being one for Bible Sunday, and published in *The Fifth Book of Best Sermons* (Cassell, 1999).

A member of the Prayer Book Society, the College of Preachers, the Hymn Society, the Lambeth Association and the Walsingham Association, Dr Critchlow – when not preaching – divides her time between lecturing and writing, editing and translating for Russian Christians. She is involved in the running and preparation of lectures in a Bible College near the Siberian–Mongolian border, training pastors for both countries; and, on the home front, she is a churchwarden, parochial church councillor, and a member of the deanery synod.

Preaching on the Common Worship Lectionary

A RESOURCE BOOK

To
DINAH,
whose friendship, courage and faith
sustain and inspire
in times of trauma and joy –
and whose ministry hopefully will,
in God's good time,
also extend to the pulpit

Published in Great Britain in 2000 by
Society for Promoting Christian Knowledge
Holy Trinity Church, Marylebone Road, London NW1 4DU

British Library Cataloguing-in-Publication Data

A catalogue record for this book is available from the British Library

ISBN 0-281-05256-5

Typeset by Wilmaset Ltd, Birkenhead, Wirral

Printed in Great Britain by The Cromwell Press, Trowbridge, Wiltshire

Contents

Acknowledgements

I wish to express my gratitude to the many theologians – both clerical and lay – who have been God's instrument in persuading me to pursue Theology, and who subsequently encouraged me to hope that the Church of England would survive my admittance to its pulpits.

I should also like to thank most sincerely Alison Barr, commissioning editor at SPCK, and Linda Crosby, copy-editor, for their generous help and expertise in seeing the manuscript through from idea to completion.

Any shortcomings herein are entirely my own.

INTRODUCTION

Preaching: Approach and Technique

The aim

The preacher may believe that he or she is one of God's greatest gifts
to mankind, but the congregation may take a little more convincing;
also, listeners will soon become disillusioned unless the unadulterated,
unvarnished way to God through Christ is preached from the pulpit.
That, basically, is why preachers are there: to be the mouthpiece of
God, and to give worshippers encouragement on their spiritual
journey. A preacher's command is no earthly command. We are
dealing not only with heavenly things in an earthly setting, but with
the indefinable: that which will survive death itself. Jesus has promised:
'Heaven and earth will pass away, but my words will not pass away'
(Mark 13.31).

So how does one define or classify a sermon? The answer is, with
great difficulty indeed, because sermons depend on individuals, traditions, time or place; they may be catholic or evangelical; expository or
biographical; of local interest or wider impact; precisely structured or
extempore. Some congregations have the stamina for a 40-minute
homily, while the tolerance of others reaches danger levels after about
five minutes. Yet whatever the challenge, aim to make your main point
clearly at the outset, bend it gently into the backbone of the sermon,
and give it the full spiritual neon-light focus at the end. It works – in
theory!

The proclamation

As preachers of the gospel of Jesus, Jesus should predominate in every
sermon. As his ambassadors, we are instruments of service between God
and his people. Just as challenge as well as encouragement played key
roles in Jesus' preaching, we too need them in good measure. Our
challenge is that only by God's grace, with his call to minister, dare we
proclaim his gospel; our encouragement is that his grace is inexhaus-
tible. We, in turn, challenge our listeners: not by preaching *at* them, but
by sharing the invitation to aim for the impossible ideal that the gospel
presents – believing that God can still make all things possible. And we

encourage by reflecting on what God has so far accomplished – in our lives, and in the lives of others.

Illustrations

Stories, word-pictures and anecdotes can be of great value if used in moderation, but should not predominate in a sermon. No listener should be left remembering an illustration at the expense of the message. Listeners will usually take the line of least resistance, and will latch on to whatever is easiest to understand. But we must remember we are dealing with the word of God – not engaged in after-dinner entertainment.

Sense and sensibility

It may be relatively easy to home in on the intellect, imagination and emotions of one's local congregation. If one is preaching in another church, though, then more perception is called for. There are 'high (catholic), medium and low (evangelical)' churches within Anglicanism itself, and a variety of other combinations, all of which can present the preacher with a real challenge – especially in the case of eucharistic and major festival sermons. As a rule of thumb, avoid over-simplification: listeners more readily tend to accept mind-stretching than the feeling that they are being patronized.

Language

Clear diction and wide-ranging, understandable vocabulary are essential. Listeners will readily 'tune out' if they cannot hear or comprehend what is being heard. Speak a little slower than normal, and avoid dropping the voice at the end of a sentence. Vary the pitch: a dead-pan delivery is an invitation to boredom. Some churches have clip-on lapel microphones, which may need switching off for the sermon if the pulpit is separately 'miked'. When preaching in a different church, check with the churchwarden before the service on the PA system in use; most churchwardens will vouchsafe the information, and a few will give the preacher credit for a doctorate in mind-reading.

If preaching from notes, learn to scan ahead so that the maximum amount of eye contact with the listeners can be maintained. This also monitors any tendency for people to search for the next hymn or to unwrap sweets, or – perish the thought – to take forty winks. If any such is detected, take appropriate action by turning up the volume of delivery, changing the subject or, in extremis, concluding the sermon.

Evocative phrases, tautology in moderation – possibly even slang – can be of value not only in emphasizing a point, but in regaining lapsed attention.

The beginning and the end

These should be complementary. It is a common fault to end at a destination out of sight from the starting-point. Gain, and then set the seal on, people's attention with a dramatic, unusual, autobiographical, local or topical start. Build up gradually, to the climax of your sermon, leaving the listeners in no doubt as to the point you wish them to carry away for the rest of the week. You may decide to end on a question raised by the sermon material, which you will answer – or, at least, pursue – in the following Sunday's sermon.

One lay minister in the Derbyshire moorlands' chapels used to say of his sermons: 'I tell 'em what I'm going to tell 'em, and then I tell 'em, and then I tell 'em what I've told 'em.' In moderation, this is not a bad policy!

Delivering what has been promised

However you set your pitch at the start, the issues raised will need to be dealt with in order. A point left unfinished will leave the listeners with the choice of floundering, or setting off on their own train of thought. Try to keep to a coherent explanation or exploration of your theme, dealing adequately with each point before going on to the next. Remember that most of your listeners will not live with their Bibles open as much as you need to.

The Bible is for today

I have heard preachers say: 'I don't preach on the Bible – my congregation are not ready for it.' One wonders when they will be considered ready. Remember, it is *always* possible to apply the biblical texts to life today. Human nature does not change; and circumstances – however complicated – continue to arise from timeless factors. People in past centuries shared the need that modern folk have: to seek, and find, God. Today's preachers follow in the footsteps of giants such as Moses, Isaiah, Peter and Paul. Some of those who listen to us may also, in time, feel called to take up this challenge.

How important is feedback

Responsorial sermons – that is, where the congregation is encouraged to dialogue with the preacher – have their place, but they need to be used with discretion. In many churches, a reluctance to dialogue is still prevalent – both among preachers, and listeners. However, if it is introduced without warning, or randomly, it can do more harm than good. There are no ground rules for congregational response, though it is generally found where the evangelical persuasion is strongest.

Personal profile

1 Teacher v. learners, or *servus servorum*? No congregation likes to be preached *at*, so it is important to try to get spiritually alongside one's listeners. There should be an implicit rapport – a sharing of common truths and principles – rather than the sermon being merely an exercise in didactic.

2 How much do you give of yourself? Preaching needs to be from the heart as well as the head. We are not superhuman, six feet above the congregation (though of course we are dealing with a superhuman message), but instead are vulnerable, seeking, co-committed disciples. Each preacher develops his own style, construction and content. One of the North Country parsons of a century ago used to begin each sermon by thanking God for the weather: not always an easy task in the Derbyshire Peak District. His congregation used to wait with extra interest to hear how he would thank God for some of the weather they experienced. One Sunday in early February, the day was as bad as anyone could remember, with hard frost, blizzards and no heat in the church. 'Dear Lord,' the preacher began, to red-eyed and blue-lipped attention, 'we thank Thee for this Sabbath-day; but we thank Thee also that the weather's not often this bad! Amen.'

3 Body language can help or hinder our message. Mannerisms that detract may need to be diplomatically pointed out by a spouse or trusted friend, and then eliminated. On the other hand, a flat, ram-rod delivery with no accentuation marks can be counter-productive. Some pulpits allow for a generous amount of movement; others are a challenge even for the athletic. Beware of triple-deckers, where often the upper deck has not been used (for a variety of reasons, including safety) for decades. Beware too of candles, which can be knocked over, or singe the unwary.

4 Believe in what you are preaching. This may seem self-evident, but it is surprising how unconvincing a sermon can sound from the pews.

Without conviction and integrity, the best-prepared sermon will be little more than an exercise in semantics. *Preaching needs prayer*, to bring in (and out) the spiritual dimension that elevates it above secular communication.

A preacher's prayer:

> Lord, you have given me an awesome responsibility, in calling me to preach your word. I pray that no one seeking Christ will be hindered by any fault of mine. The voice may be human, but let the message be divine – and to you be all the glory. In Christ's name. Amen.

ADVENT

❖ **The First Sunday of Advent** YEAR A

Isa. 2.1–5; Ps. 122; Rom. 13.11–14; Matt. 24.36–44

THE PROVING GROUND

From the epistle: 'The night is far gone, the day is near. Let us then lay aside the works of darkness and put on the armour of light.' (Rom. 13.12) Who has not experienced the arrival of guests when the house is at its untidiest, the dishwasher has broken down, or there is a power cut? Well, we may usher the unexpected company into the least chaotic room, resurrect Granny's teaset from the china cabinet, and entertain by candlelight ... But what if it was the Lord who had rung our doorbell? Should we have time for such emergency measures?

Our Advent readings virtually give us a checklist of preparations, so that the divine summons may not find us totally unprepared. Let's go to God's house, where for a while we can leave the darkness of the world's pressures, and benefit from the light of the gospel in worship. Let's live as honestly as we can, following Jesus' example. We are not to worry about the Last Day (for only God knows when it will be), but instead we are to expect it, and to live as those who will one day die – that is, *really* live. Advent prepares us for Christmas: earthly life for eternity. We are to put on the armour of light to cross the proving ground: beyond this, we shall not need it.

➷

The First Sunday of Advent YEAR B

Isa. 64.1–9; Ps. 80.1–7, 17–19; 1 Cor. 1.3–9; Mark 13.24–37

INHERITORS

From the epistle: 'Just as the testimony of Christ has been strengthened among you – so that you are not lacking in any spiritual gift as you wait for the revealing of our Lord Jesus Christ.' (1 Cor. 1.6–7)

In the same way that beneficiaries receive their legacies on the death of the testator, so at Calvary, as Jesus' covenant (will, testament) was sealed in blood, we came into our Christian inheritance: the name of Jesus, the gifts of the Spirit, the armour of God. We do not have to wait until we die: we shall not be fighting Satan in heaven.

God is no niggardly giver. Paul tells us that if we lack any spiritual gift, then the fault is not with God; the onus is on us to draw on all the reserves he has given us – which are certain to exceed those that we think we have. God could make it easy for us to use our gifts, but where would the challenge be? The resurrection of Jesus could have happened in such a world-shattering way that no one was left in doubt. Instead, Jesus had to work hard on Easter Day to persuade even his closest friends that the unbelievable had happened.

But then, on Easter Day, the disciples had yet to receive the Holy Spirit.

$$\approx$$

The First Sunday of Advent   YEAR C

Jer. 33.14–16; Ps. 25.1–10; 1 Thess. 3.9–13; Luke 21.25–36

AS GOD INTENDS

From the epistle: 'How can we thank God enough for you in return for all the joy that we feel before our God because of you?' (1 Thess. 3.9)

We are usually far better at asking God for help than thanking him for what he has done: at interceding for friends, rather than simply giving thanks for them. Jesus tells us not to let worries and their ilk weigh us down. The *Amplified Bible* renders John 14.27 as: 'Stop allowing yourselves to be agitated and disturbed; and do not permit yourselves to be fearful and intimidated and cowardly and unsettled.' The antidote to worry is praise and thanksgiving. Have I a problem? Let me share it – with God, with a friend. It is only by cutting our worries down that we can release our minds to function as God intends.

James Hudson Taylor, in the outback of China, received bad news of a couple of fellow-missionaries. He began whistling his favourite hymn: 'Jesus, I am resting, resting in the joy of what Thou art'. 'How can you think of hymns when you've just had such bad news?' his assistant asked in amazement. 'Why should I not?' Taylor replied. 'Giving way to worry will not help them, and will unfit me for service.'

❖ The Second Sunday of Advent YEAR A

Isa. 11.1–10; Ps. 72.1–7, 18–19; Rom. 15.4–13; Matt. 3.1–12

GOD'S WORD

From the epistle: 'For whatever was written in former days was written for our instruction.' (Rom. 15.4)

For many of us, this second Sunday of Advent still means 'Bible Sunday', when Bibles of many languages are taken to church, and worshippers join in prayer for Christians around the world. Our readings emphasize this cosmic theme – from the time of God's promises to the patriarchs, to the ushering in of his peaceful kingdom where nations will not know war, and glory will fill the earth. Meanwhile, we are to try to live in peace with one another. God's love is boundless: the nations, creeds and cultures on earth may ignore it, but they cannot exhaust it.

Jesus quoted from the old scriptures many times; this is particularly seen in John's Gospel. We, too, are to learn from the past. God's word can never become obsolete; the commission to take the gospel worldwide has never been revoked. Do we share God's truths with as many as we can, in all the ways we can, while we can? Let us remember St Jerome, William Tyndale, and all who have devoted their lives to translating the Bible into the language of their times.

෨

The Second Sunday of Advent YEAR B

Isa. 40.1–11; Ps. 85.1–2, 8–13; 2 Pet. 3.8–15a; Mark 1.1–8

GOD'S PATIENCE

From the epistle: 'The Lord is not slow about his promise, as some think of slowness, but is patient with you, not wanting any to perish, but all to come to repentance.' (2 Pet. 3.9)

As the psalmist had realized, the Lord is on our side (Ps. 118.6). God does not strive against us – and what a mercy that he does not, or no one would have a chance. Though he may seem slow in coming to our help, he comes in time. With our pedestrian reckoning of seconds, minutes and hours, we have a poor understanding of God's time.

Tertullian used to pray for patience, but God patiently gave his fiery preacher a free rein against the pagans:

If the Tiber reaches the walls,
If the Nile doesn't rise to the fields,
If the sky doesn't move, or the earth does,
If there is famine, if there is plague,
The cry is at once: 'The Christians to the lion!'
What – all of them, to one lion?

(Tertullian, *Apology*, 40.20)

Isaiah, John and Jesus were men of their time, in the timeless patience of God's planning. We need to read our present, in the light of God's past, and to accept God's direction of the future.

ॐ

The Second Sunday of Advent   YEAR C

Baruch 5.1–9 or Mal. 3.1–4; *Canticle*: Benedictus; Phil. 1.3–11; Luke 3.1–6

GOOD NEWS

From the apocrypha: 'Take off the garment of your sorrow and affliction, O Jerusalem, and put on forever the beauty of the glory from God.' (Baruch 5.1)

This is not an instruction to exchange grief for ephemeral joy, but to make a lasting, quality decision never to return to despair. John emphasizes the need for immediacy: while we delay, the opportunity may be lost.

We are not quick learners. Two millennia after the light of Jesus came with hope and joy, we still apparently love to wallow in gloom and despair. Bad news grabs the headlines. Most people are sad – due to grief, worry, sickness or loneliness. Can we, this Advent, do something to redress the balance – we, who would have an abundance of Christ's joy in our hearts, we, his ambassadors, under a precious obligation to show Christ to a world in need of him?

'Forever' is a long day, but God's joy is long enough to last for it increases with the spreading. And it differs from mere happiness in that it is not a feeling, but rather a state of being; we may not feel joyful, but in God we can still be joyful. We may think of a thousand other ways of living; but only by taking the joy of God to others and sharing it with them can we be said to be really alive in Christ.

❖ The Third Sunday of Advent

Isa. 35.1–10; Ps. 146.5–10 or *Canticle*: Magnificat; Jas. 5.7–10; Matt. 11.2–11

ATTENDING TO GOD

From the gospel: 'Are you the one who is to come, or are we to wait for another?' (Matt. 11.3)

We hear of people waiting so long for a bus or train that when the vehicle eventually comes, they allow it to pass unnoticed. We may smile at the story – until it happens to us, and then we are too embarrassed to share the experience.

'Be patient', Jesus counsels. But it is to be a watchful patience, an expectancy that cherishes the promises of men like Isaiah and the psalmist; a watchfulness that stays faithful, no matter how the world and its glitz tries to distract us.

John had been watchful, faithful in preaching, courageous in baptizing, fearless in opposing those who rejected his message. Yet the prison conditions at Machaerus took their toll, until doubt eventually came between him and his faith in Jesus.

Had he really waited so long that he had missed a signpost somewhere? Why was God allowing his messenger to languish in prison? Surely, if Jesus was the Messiah . . . ? John's lapse of attention warns us that ours, too, can be deflected – whether at the bus stop or in the line of Christian duty.

∂⸚

The Third Sunday of Advent

Isa. 61.1–4, 8–11; Ps. 126 or *Canticle*: Magnificat; 1 Thess. 5.16–24; John 1.6–8, 19–28

BE THANKFUL

From the epistle: 'Rejoice always, pray without ceasing, give thanks in all circumstances; for this is the will of God in Christ Jesus for you.' (1 Thess. 5.16–18)

It's hard to meet every day as a challenge, giving thanks to God in all circumstances, welcoming the opportunity of climbing to the next rung on a ladder that threatens to collapse at any minute. But it has to be done. The alternative is: become mediocre, join the crowd on a hiding to nothing. The world understands mediocrity: it's next door to ordinariness.

> In the world's broad field of battle,
> In the bivouac of life,
> Be not like dumb, driven cattle,
> Be a hero in the strife!
> Trust no Future, howe'er pleasant!
> Let the dead Past bury its dead!
> Act – act in the living Present!
> Heart within, and God o'erhead!
> (H. W. Longfellow)

If circumstances are threatening our joy, we can ask: are we in the will of God today? If we seem to be further from God than we used to be, then can we be quite sure it isn't God who has moved?

☙

The Third Sunday of Advent   YEAR C

Zeph. 3.14–20; *Canticle*: Isa. 12.2–6; Phil. 4.4–7; Luke 3.7–18

WORRY NOT

From the prophets: 'The LORD has taken away the judgments against you, he has turned away your enemies. The king of Israel, the LORD, is in your midst; you shall fear disaster no more.' (Zeph. 3.15)

'Do not worry about anything' – Paul builds on the confidence of Zephaniah. Let us take heed. We have become so proficient in worrying. Have we forgotten that it is unchristian? Even in the run-up to one of the most joyful festivals of the year, we worry about extraneous details until the Christ-Child goes virtually unnoticed.

But God is on our side. Look how he operates, taking away adverse judgements, turning away foes. He is here among us. Don't be afraid! The power in us is greater than anything that is outside us (1 John 4.4); and all it needs is that step of faith to begin the change from despair to hope. No one is going to do it for us. We are not to waste time praying for God to give us his Spirit; the Spirit has already been given. Why do we choose to let him rest in us unused? If we pray him to work through us in every situation, we open the door for God to use us in ways we could never have imagined were possible.

❖ The Fourth Sunday of Advent YEAR A

Isa. 7.10–16; Ps. 80.1–7, 17–19; Rom. 1.1–7; Matt. 1.18–25

IMPOSSIBLE!

From the prophets: 'The Lord himself will give you a sign. Look, the young woman is with child ... Immanuel [God is with us].' (Isa. 7.14)

An American philanthropist, having read a book of modern sermons, invited each of the preachers for a week's holiday at his Jamaican home. Nearly half of the recipients consigned his letter to the wastepaper-basket, thinking it was a joke.

How often we let the unexpected take us unawares! If we do not see it on the screen, or in the papers, we treat the unusual with scant regard.

The prophets who foretold Jesus' birth, and Joseph who responded to the angel's stunning news with quiet dignity, have much to teach us about the unexpected workings of God. Can we, as Christmas beckons, set aside the tinsel and instead try to see this miraculous event through the eyes of Joseph, Mary, the shepherds and the Magi?

What should we have done? Knelt in worship, or considered the news to be outrageously impossible? God still reserves the right to do the impossible. He still leaves it to us, in faith, to move the mountains.

૭

The Fourth Sunday of Advent YEAR B

2 Sam. 7.1–11, 16; *Canticle*: Magnificat or Ps. 89.1–4, 19–26; Rom. 16.25–27; Luke 1.26–38

MY GOSPEL?

From the epistle: 'Now to God who is able to strengthen you according to my gospel and the proclamation of Jesus Christ.' (Rom. 16.25)

Paul has already referred to 'my gospel' (Rom. 2.16); now he reiterates this lovely truth. Can we be so confident? Or do we preach, or attend worship, to teach or to hear *a* gospel? We need fellowship with Christ as a personal Friend. True, he is God – but even Satan knows him as that; and angels worship him as King. How close are we to Jesus?

God is able, and willing, to strengthen us, the more we proclaim Jesus. Peter and the earliest disciples knew the power of Jesus' name, which could save (Acts 2.38) and heal (Acts 3.16). It was this name that the newly converted Paul was commissioned to bring 'before Gentiles and kings and before the people of Israel' (Acts 9.15). By no other name is salvation possible (Acts 4.12).

We are just days away from Christmas. Christ's name will be on the lips of many who do not normally acknowledge him. Can we pray that true recognition will come for these people? Can we resolve to share *our* gospel with as many folk as we can, to make their Christmas real?

᙮

The Fourth Sunday of Advent   YEAR C
Mic. 5.2–5a; *Canticle*: Magnificat or Ps. 80.1–7; Heb. 10.5–10; Luke 1.39–45[46–55]

HUMILITY

From the gospel: 'He has looked with favour on the lowliness of his servant. Surely, from now on all generations will call me blessed.' (Luke 1.48)

God had not looked on beauty, wealth, high position, intellectual attainment – but on Mary's humility. As the ostentatiousness of a modern Christmas approaches, may we reflect on God's choice of the woman at the centre of the celebration.

His favour did not change Mary, but it marked her out for ever. Even in our bustle and rush, can we find time to reflect on why God has chosen us? Perhaps we have since given him cause to reverse his decision! That he has kept faith with us must surely add to our joy this Christmas.

Yes, 'the wise may bring their learning', and the rich their gold – and if we are included here, we cannot come to Jesus empty-handed. But whatever our station, let us bring him those 'hearts that love him, and thankful praise', which counts for more than intellect or wealth.

He may meet us as the Child in the manger, but he has also been through Calvary. He is also Very God.

CHRISTMAS

❖ **Christmas Eve** YEARS A, B, C

2 Sam. 7.1–5, 8–11, 16; Ps. 89.2, 21–27; Acts 13.16–26; Luke 1.67–79

HOMELESS

From the prophets: 'Go and tell my servant David: Thus says the LORD: Are you the one to build me a house to live in?' (2 Sam. 7.5)

Babies who come into the world at inconvenient times – perhaps on a bus or train, or in a theatre, or even during a church service – often make the news. Readers, it seems, never tire of hearing about a birth that is unconventional. What would the 'Bethlehem Gazette' have made of Jesus' birth? How would reporters have coped with details of an angelic visitation from simple shepherds?

Conceived out of wedlock, born in a cattle-shed, Jesus – thirty or so years ahead – will lie in a borrowed tomb. Even foxes and birds had a place to call their own (Luke 9.58). Yet today much of the world is celebrating the birth of this little homeless stranger, who came to give, not to receive: to give enough joy and love for the world, and to spare.

Let us, today, give out this joy and love of Christmas, looking – as did Jesus – for nothing in return.

❖ **Christmas Day** YEAR A

Isa. 9.2–7; Ps. 96; Titus 2.11–14; Luke 2.1–14[15–20]

MORE THAN A CHILD

From the prophets: 'For a child has been born for us, a son given to us; authority rests upon his shoulders; and he is named Wonderful Counsellor, Mighty God, Everlasting Father, Prince of Peace.' (Isa. 9.6)

We stand, by the grace of God, *in loco parentis*: a son has been given to us. By a divine alchemy we cannot hope to fathom, we are to Jesus as his mother, brothers and sisters. Mary, with love and great dignity, somehow came to terms with being the mother of her Creator. We can do no less.

As Wonderful Counsellor, he guides us into all truth: first as Man while he was on earth, and then through his Holy Spirit. As Mighty God, he has all authority in heaven and on earth: wherever Satan tries to operate, he is trespassing on Christian territory. As Everlasting Father, God claims us as his children for ever. And as the Prince of Peace, his will is behind us in every peaceable endeavour.

As we meet the Child in the manger this morning, he is all this, and more; how much more, only our hearts can tell us.

And, as they tell us, it is then our mission to pass on the good news.

❧

Christmas Day   YEAR B
Isa. 62.6–12; Ps. 97; Titus 3.4–7; Luke 2.[1–7] 8–20

A FREE GIFT

From the epistle: 'But when the goodness and loving kindness of God our Saviour appeared, he saved us, not because any works of righteousness that we had done, but according to his mercy, through the water of rebirth and renewal by the Holy Spirit.' (Titus 3.4–5)

Dr Billy Graham has said: 'Salvation is free, but discipleship costs.' And if it does not cost, how committed is our allegiance to Christ? As Christians, we share Christmas with millions of unbelievers. If they cannot accept the gift Jesus brings, what can we do? If today is no more than a time of pleasure and freedom from work, how can we make a difference that matters in their lives?

Christmas is about caring enough to make the effort. Everyone loves to be loved, and having a friend who has faith in you means more than anything else. Every Christian has been chosen by a God who has faith that one day we shall realize our full spiritual potential. Our mission, in turn, is not to muscle in on anyone else's potential, but to alert others to the truth that they have a special potential of their own to realize.

❧

Christmas Day

Isa. 52.7–10; Ps. 98; Heb. 1.1–4[5–12]; John 1.1–14

TO HIS OWN

From the gospel: 'He came to what was his own, and his own people did not accept him.' (John 1.11)

God knew what his people were expecting: a king to rule and prosper, a high priest to occupy the holy of holies, and a messiah to come in glory.

So Jesus came, and people's faith was tested. Ecclesiastical scholarship failed the test, and Jesus was worshipped by simple shepherds and Gentile professors.

He comes yet again today. Who are the shepherds and professors of this Christmas?

We who greet Jesus this morning surely dare not come without gifts for our Lord: a heart of love, a mind on fire to seek further into his will, a soul of thankfulness for his many gifts – but chiefly, today of all days, for himself. Whether we have led a few or many to him in recent weeks, let us resolve to allow God to see to their salvation, as we continue to share his word with more and more: for, as 'there is no longer Jew or Greek ... slave or free ... male and female', we are all 'one in Christ Jesus' (Gal. 3.28), we are all 'his own'. Christ never compels – but he still invites. RSVP.

❖ The First Sunday of Christmas

Isa. 63.7–9; Ps. 148; Heb. 2.10–18; Matt. 2.13–23

STANDING THE TEST

From the epistle: 'Because he himself was tested by what he suffered, he is able to help those who are being tested.' (Heb. 2.18)

Testing so often breeds introspectiveness, and we tell ourselves (and anyone else within earshot) that no one else knows how we are suffering: no one has ever been through our particular test before – we are unmindful of the fact that our monologue is unbiblical, and that we are virtually saying that we are so special that Christ's incarnation and testing was not good enough for us.

The wrapping may alter with the centuries, but human nature

remains essentially the same; and the core of our testing, when the glitz has been stripped off, is akin to the testing that Jesus met and overcame some two millennia ago.

Does illness, poverty, worry, doubt or any other trauma test you just now? Of course it does, because you are human. But God is able to help. Corrie ten Boom, the Dutch evangelist, sometimes told herself: 'Corrie, this thing over which you are worrying right now is too big for you; in fact, it's too big for God to handle!' And, as the absurdity of these last words sank in, she would have to laugh. It works!

The testing may not seem to impose too much on Christmas Day. But God is able, every day.

પ

The First Sunday of Christmas YEAR B

Isa. 61.10—62.3; Ps. 148; Gal. 4.4–7; Luke 2.15–21

DADDY!

From the epistle: 'And because you are children, God has sent the Spirit of his Son into our hearts, crying, "Abba! Father!"' (Gal. 4.6)

A healthy respect for God is obligatory: he is the Almighty Creator. But Jesus showed us the essential Fatherhood of God: intimate, loving, caring – and, above all, approachable. We are not, even metaphorically, expected to crawl into his presence on hands and knees, begging for a crumb of mercy, but 'with a true heart in full assurance of faith' (Heb. 10.22).

I know that my Redeemer lives!
What joy the blessed assurance gives!
(Samuel Medley, 1738–99)

Getting close to God as 'Abba' ('Daddy') takes practice – just as we have to learn to grow into a close relationship with our earthly fathers. 'Abba' recognizes no time, no space. The child of three, and the centenarian, can both fellowship with 'Abba'. Read the long prayer of Jesus to his 'Abba' in John 17, and take it as a model for your own relationship with God – remembering that God also loves to joy. He has not given us a sense of humour for our benefit alone!

પ

The First Sunday of Christmas YEAR C

1 Sam. 2.18–20, 26; Ps. 148; Col. 3.12–17; Luke 2.41–52

GROWING UP

From the gospel: 'Jesus increased in wisdom and in years, and in divine and human favour.' (Luke 2.52)

We know that Jesus was never out of God's will, but this verse ends on an intriguing note. Was he popular in Nazareth? Surely he must have been – until he returned as an accomplished preacher and worker of miracles. We also can gain 'human favour' – until, that is, we stand out for God: then the world appears to have a problem in accepting us. But if, like Jesus, our (godly) wisdom has increased with the years, then – like Jesus – we shall accept the loss of human favour with equanimity. It is not our loss: the people who rejected Jesus forfeited his miracles (Mark 6.5).

When we are growing up, it can often seem indispensable to have human favour: it helps in getting a job, making friends, establishing one's 'circle'. If we can accomplish this without compromising our standing with God, all well and good. But if, in any part of our growing up, we are growing away from God, if we ask him in prayer he will bring the deviation to our notice – very gently, until we have attended to it.

❖ The Second Sunday of Christmas YEARS A, B, C

(Principal service readings for Years A, B and C are the same.)
Jer. 31.7–14 or Ecclus. 24.1–12; Ps. 147.12–20 or *Canticle*: Wisd. 10.15–21; Eph. 1.3–14; John 1.[1–9]10–18

BETTER THAN THE LAW

From the gospel: 'The law indeed was given through Moses; grace and truth came through Jesus Christ.' (John 1.17)

It is not easy to live according to a set of laws, but it is easier than living in the grace and truth of Jesus. Manmade laws – and even God-given laws in Mosaic times – are set between parameters: at times set fairly close, at other times further apart. But Jesus brought a new dimension in his message of grace and truth: 'You have heard that it was said to those of ancient times, ... But I say to you' (Matt. 5.21–22a). It is all of a piece with his sending out of the first missionaries: ' "When I sent you out without a purse, bag, or sandals, did you lack anything?" ... "But now, the one who has a purse must take it, and likewise a bag" ' (Luke 22.35–36a). Whether it was on divorce, or the Deuteronomic 'eye for eye', Jesus brought his new interpretation to bear.

Too hard? An impossible ideal? He simply tells us that nothing is impossible with God. Yes, it may seem impossible to us: and, in the natural, it is. But Jesus mixes our efforts with his amalgam of grace and truth until our initial endeavours have been transformed beyond recognition. Impossible – but better than the law!

EPIPHANY

❖ The Epiphany YEARS A, B, C

Isa. 60.1–6; Ps. 72.[1–9]10–15; Eph. 3.1–12; Matt. 2.1–12

WORLDWIDE INHERITORS

From the epistle: 'The Gentiles have become fellow heirs, members of the same body, and sharers in the promise in Christ Jesus through the gospel.' (Eph. 3.6)

From Davidic and Isaianic times, the Jews had known that one day the Gentiles would inherit God's promises. Yet when Jesus came, they were slow to believe that that time had come. We cling to privilege and power, freedom and faith, as if we have a monopoly on it: this is not God's outlook. Whatever we have is a gift from him, a gift to be shared. Today, as we focus on the Magi – the pains they took to come to Jesus, the gifts they brought, and the generosity of spirit that led them to worship a child of another faith – can we take stock of how we are sharing with others what God has given us?

We may have talents, possessions and money: these are the first that come to mind; but we all have time as well, and often it is in making time for others that the greatest joy is found. It seems as if our world today is short of time, yet there are still as many hours in each day as there were in the days of Jesus, Paul, Isaiah and David.

❖ The Baptism of Christ YEAR A
(The First Sunday of Epiphany)

Isa. 42.1–9; Ps. 29; Acts 10.34–43; Matt. 3.13–17

SPIRIT-ANOINTED

From the epistle: 'That message spread throughout Judea, beginning in Galilee after the baptism that John announced: how God anointed Jesus of Nazareth with the Holy Spirit and with power; how he went about doing good and healing all who were oppressed by the devil, for God was with him.' (Acts 10.37–38)

Jesus was at pains to improve the quality of life for people on earth, freeing them from devilish encumbrances such as sickness and disease, to serve God better in the pre-eternal proving-time. He had no hesitation in ascribing physical disability to Satan (Luke 13.16), sending a clear answer to those who assumed (and to any who still assume) that God sends illness to test us.

God still allows illness, but he does not send it. We cannot understand why some people are healed, and others are not; but no one knows everything about another's life, and we cannot always see how our lives interrelate – or, indeed, every result that can come from an illness or disability. What we can rely on is the fact that the same Spirit-power that came on Jesus has also come on us. We can choose to use it, or not.

ತನ

The Baptism of Christ YEAR B
(The First Sunday of Epiphany)
Gen. 1.1–5; Ps. 29; Acts 19.1–7; Mark 1.4–11

DID YOU RECEIVE?
From the epistle: '[Paul] said to them: "Did you receive the Holy Spirit when you became believers?" ... When Paul had laid his hands on them, the Holy Spirit came upon them, and they spoke in tongues and prophesied.' (Acts 19.2, 6)

John had done his job faithfully, and Paul was not negating his baptism; instead he was building on it, with the additional power of the Spirit made available by Jesus. The result brought a significant enrichment to the Ephesians' ministry. We cannot evaluate the Spirit's power – only accept that it exceeds anything we can imagine.

Speaking in tongues (glossolalia) and prophesying are not exhaustively the gifts of the Spirit, and we should not feel specially excluded if they are not manifested in our particular ministry. The Spirit is given to all believers, but in ways best suited to the individual. We take the capital he gives, and use it to the best advantage, knowing our Father has tailored it to our needs as no earthly financial adviser could hope to match. Our baptism in the Spirit is the longest-term investment ever devised.

๛

The Baptism of Christ YEAR C
(The First Sunday of Epiphany)

Isa. 43.1–7; Ps. 29; Acts 8.14–17; Luke 3.15–17, 21–22

YOU ARE MINE

From the prophets: 'Do not fear, for I have redeemed you; I have called you by name, you are mine. When you pass through the waters, I will be with you; and through the rivers, they shall not overwhelm you; when you walk through fire you shall not be burned, and the flame shall not consume you.' (Isa. 43.1b–2)

Isaiah's readers would think of Moses and the Israelites at the Red Sea; later generations would think of Shadrach and his companions in the fiery furnace. God had proved capable of defying the natural laws to safeguard his own; and today destruction – even on a nuclear scale – operates only as God permits.

Can we realize the love and compassion of a God who can give us such protection and redemption, and who knows us by name? No, we cannot: we have to accept it in sheer faith. There will be wars, but many will experience unaccountable deliverance. There will be accidents, but many will not be touched by them. God alone knows why. This does not mean that our prayers are unnecessary: there are biblical precedents for prayer changing God's mind. Such is the exciting challenge he gives us!

❖ The Second Sunday of Epiphany YEAR A

Isa. 49.1–7; Ps. 40.1–11; 1 Cor. 1.1–9; John 1.29–42

CALLED AND CHOSEN

From the prophets and the epistle: 'The LORD called me before I was born ... the Holy One of Israel ... has chosen you.' (Isa. 49.1b, 7h)

'Paul, called to be an apostle ... to those ... called to be saints ... God is faithful; by him you were called into the fellowship of his Son, Jesus Christ our Lord.' (1 Cor. 1.1a, 2b, 9)

Before we were born, God had us on his mind, earmarked for royal service. He was taking a risk, because he knew he would also be allowing us the freedom of choice. This gift, the most daring of all, is probably the one we use, or misuse, the most. The more carefully we employ it, the greater is our freedom; unwise choices bind us more tightly to the restrictions of the world.

God is faithful: we have a partner in ministry who is generous in his affirmation and who will not let us down. Are we fellowshipping with others in like manner? How many people rely on us, in one way or another? Being late for meetings, or forgetting appointments, may seem little matters: but they are not in line with Christian fellowship of people called to be saints.

We may not feel saintly – but we cannot deny our calling.

❧

The Second Sunday of Epiphany   YEAR B

1 Sam. 3.1–10[11–20]; Ps. 139.1–6, 13–18; Rev. 5.1–10; John 1.43–51

SAINTS FROM ALL NATIONS

From the epistle: 'They sing a new song: "You are worthy to take the scroll and open its seals, for you were slaughtered and by your blood you ransomed for God saints from every tribe and language and people and nation; you have made them to be a kingdom and priests serving our God, and they will reign on earth." ' (Rev. 5.9–10)

Of the 6,000 languages on earth, the Bible (or parts of it) has been translated into just over a third; and while many of the remainder are minority tongues, it nevertheless means that there are still many people and nations who have yet to hear the word of God: many possible saints who are still ignorant of their inheritance; many singers who do not yet know the 'new song' of God.

We can reach out to these unreached – in prayer. We can send finances to support Bible translators. We can answer the call of mission and go to spread the gospel in far-off countries. We can do all these – or none of them. The choice is ours.

But can we look at the Bible in our churches, and on our bookshelves at home, and imagine what our lives would be like without God's word?

❧

The Second Sunday of Epiphany YEAR C

Isa. 62.1–5; Ps. 36.5–10; 1 Cor. 12.1–11; John 2.1–11

THE SPIRIT'S VOICE

From the epistle: 'You know that when you were pagans, you were enticed and led astray to idols that could not speak ... To one is given through the Spirit the utterance of wisdom, and to another the utterance of knowledge according to the same Spirit.' (1 Cor. 12.2, 8)

Paul points to a major difference between dumb pagan idols and the eloquently vocal Spirit of God. Jesus emphasized the importance of words, and had uncomfortable things to say about the judging of every idle word. James speaks at length about the power of the tongue.

A Christian's words should be full of spiritual wisdom, seasoned with gospel-salt. Each day, hundreds of thousands of words waft into the ether, and affect others' lives – for good or bad. Let us resolve to weigh our words, to pray for godly guidance in the choice of them; and to value the tongue as a front-line weapon in the fight against evil.

❖ The Third Sunday of Epiphany YEAR A

Isa. 9.1–4; Ps. 27.1, 4–9; 1 Cor. 1.10–18; Matt. 4.12–23

IN ACCORD

From the epistle: 'Now I appeal to you, brothers and sisters, by the name of our Lord Jesus Christ, that all of you be in agreement and that there be no divisions among you, but that you be united in the same mind and the same purpose.' (1 Cor. 1.10)

Light for darkness, accord for discord: such is the transformation faith brings; and if we are really business-like in our commitment, our light and accord will impress upon many other lives.

The world looks askance at the Church, because at times we simplify its perplexity by our divisions and differences. The cause of Christian unity needs to be advanced in this new millennium, so the Church's voice is both respected and heard in a world that gets noisier by the year.

The *Amplified Bible*'s rendering of 1 Cor. 13.4–8 could beneficially be taken as our vade-mecum, in particular v. 5: 'Love ... is not touchy or fretful or resentful; it takes no account of the evil done to it – pays no attention to a suffered wrong.'

In his three-year ministry on earth, Jesus was a walking example of love. The Church has had far longer to set a similar example; it is still working on it.

è

The Third Sunday of Epiphany   YEAR B
Gen. 14.17–20; Ps. 128; Rev. 19.6–10; John 2.1–11

ROYAL MARRIAGE

From the epistle: 'Hallelujah! For the Lord our God the Almighty reigns. Let us rejoice and exult and give him the glory, for the marriage of the Lamb has come, and his bride has made herself ready.' (Rev. 19. 6b, 7)

That Jesus' first recorded miracle was at a marriage-feast is significant, for it foreshadowed the greater celebration between Christ and his bride, the Church. In the same way that a bride traditionally promises to obey her husband, so the Church is bound to Christ by obedience and mutual love. As husband and wife are not two, but one, so the Church is indissolubly linked and one with Christ. As a husband gives his name to his bride, so Christ has given us his name, and the power and blessing that go with it. As husband and wife come together for procreation, so the fusion of Christ and his Church nurtures succeeding generations of Christians.

How real is this royal marriage to us? How conscious are we that, in all we are, do, say and everywhere we go, we are presenting Christ, our spouse, to the world? The awesomeness of the responsibility is exceeded only by the glory of the privilege. 'Hallelujah! For the Lord our God the Almighty reigns!'

è

The Third Sunday of Epiphany YEAR C

Neh. 8.1–3, 5–6, 8–10; Ps. 19; 1 Cor. 12.12–31a; Luke 4.14–21

TODAY IS HOLY

From the prophets: 'Then [Nehemiah] said to them, "Go your way, eat the fat and drink sweet wine and send portions of them to those for whom nothing is prepared, for this day is holy to our LORD; and do not be grieved, for the joy of the LORD is your strength."' (Neh. 8.10)

Yesterday is but a dream, and tomorrow may not come. We are to live each day as fully as we can, believing that God will give us strength (= joy) sufficient for that day.

Nehemiah's labourers worked hard to rebuild the walls of Jerusalem. At times the opposition was so intense that some men would work with a tool in one hand and a weapon in the other. Such concentrated energy can only last so long, and Nehemiah was wise enough to know when to call a Holy Day. The Christian life is real and earnest, but one day in every seven is allowed by God for the sheer joy of worship and relaxation.

When we get to the stage where the two are synonymous, we are not far from the kingdom of God. Today, let us assess our God-given strength, and thereby evaluate our particular joy in our Lord.

❖ The Fourth Sunday of Epiphany YEAR A

1 Kings 17.8–16; Ps. 36.5–10; 1 Cor. 1.18–31; John 2.1–11

FOUNTAIN OF LIFE

From the prophets: 'Thus says the LORD the God of Israel: The jar of meal will not be emptied and the jug of oil will not fail until the day that the LORD sends rain on the earth.' (1 Kings 17.14)

God's resources do not dry up. At times, like the widow of Zarephath, we may be taken to what we think is the limit of endurance; but God will not allow us to go beyond our limit (1 Cor. 10.13). Like an athlete determined to press through the pain-barrier to convert mediocrity to excellence, we are to power our way through from faith to greater faith.

It was as the psalmist pictured God's vast resources as the 'fountain of life' that light dawned on his understanding (Ps. 36.9). God's bounty continues, but on earth we are used to dealing with finite riches, decreasing supplies, pleasures that come to an end. New every morning, the fountain of life wells up in us, as God's Spirit empowers us for everything the day holds in store. Can we not thrill to this daily challenge? If we have lost the ability to wonder at its freshness and vitality, something infinitely precious has gone from our hearts.

രു

The Fourth Sunday of Epiphany   YEAR B

Deut. 18.15–20; Ps. 111; Rev. 12.1–5a; Mark 1.21–28

SPIRITUAL KNOWLEDGE

From the gospel: 'Just then there was in their synagogue a man with an unclean spirit, and he cried out: "What have you to do with us, Jesus of Nazareth? Have you come to destroy us? I know who you are, the Holy One of God." ' (Mark 1.23–24)

Today's readings hint at a world with which we are unfamiliar: the world of the spirits, where there are wars and struggles that make our small terrestrial strifes puny by comparison. Perhaps our spiritual stamina is being strengthened in our time here, to fit us for an eternity that may be much more energetic and exciting than the 'sweet by and by' of our imagination!

Although many of Jesus' listeners had a problem with his identity, according to the Gospels, unclean (evil) spirits knew him straightaway. It is a warning to us that much difference lies between knowing about Jesus, and knowing him. Satan and his cohorts have known about Jesus for much longer than we have.

Let us thank our Lord that while to an evil spirit he may be recognized as 'the Holy One of God', to us he is 'Saviour, Redeemer, Friend'. Is this all?

രു

The Fourth Sunday of Epiphany   YEAR C

Ezek. 43.27—44.4; Ps. 48; 1 Cor. 13.1–13; Luke 2.22–40

LOVE'S GRADUATION

From the epistle: 'When I was a child, I spoke like a child, I thought like a child, I reasoned like a child; when I became an adult, I put an end to childish ways.' (1 Cor. 13.11)

The Christian gospel is one of growth – whether of a baby growing to manhood as Saviour of the world; a grain of wheat showing by its maturity the difference between our mortal and our resurrection bodies; or Paul's teaching here about the growth and development of love in our lives. Nothing in our physical life is static: circumstances change, and we change. Why should we try to keep our spiritual lives in Sunday School wrappings, when the Holy Spirit is waiting to lead us on to graduation – and beyond?

As in school, where our progress is largely determined by the subjects at which we do best, so in life we are developing talents that one day may be used in a wider sphere. Generally, we do best at the things we like best; let us offer these talents back to their Giver, to be used as he wishes (which may not be exactly how we think they should be used).

And let's praise God for the interest he takes in our lives. Is this interest reciprocated?

❖ Candlemas   2 February   YEARS A, B, C

Purification of the Virgin
Presentation of Christ in the Temple

Mal. 3.1–5; Ps. 24.[1–6] 7–10; Heb. 2.14–18; Luke 2.22–40

THE WORLD'S LIGHT

From the epistle: 'Therefore he had to become like his brothers and sisters in every respect, so that he might be a merciful and faithful high priest in the service of God, to make a sacrifice of atonement for the sins of the people.' (Heb. 2.17)

Although he was God, Jesus conformed to the traditions and rituals of his day: circumcision, presentation, regular synagogue-worship, baptism from John, paying tribute. Christians may stand out from the world in many ways – but Jesus' example shows us that to break with a formality purely for the sake of change is not the way of God. Paul goes more deeply into the subject in 1 Corinthians 8.

Today we light our candles to celebrate the coming of Christ's light into a world that still needs it badly – and whose need is even greater if unacknowledged. Candlemas has been observed for at least fourteen centuries, and in many churches is being rediscovered today as an important celebration of light before the long, dark fast of Lent begins.

It is a festival where old gives way to new, age to youth, as Simeon blesses the Saviour of the world, and Mary realizes ever more clearly the uniqueness of her Child.

ORDINARY TIME

❖ **Proper 1** YEAR A

Isa. 58. 1–9a [9b–12]; Ps. 112. 1–9 [10]; 1 Cor. 2.1–12 [13–16]; Matt. 5.13–20

SPIRITUAL UNDERSTANDING

From the epistle: 'No one comprehends what is truly God's except the Spirit of God. Now we have received not the spirit of the world, but the Spirit that is from God, so that we may understand the gifts bestowed on us by God.' (1 Cor. 2.11b–12)

Jesus told us that the Spirit would remind us of everything he had said, and would lead us into all truth. Paul explains that we can only understand what God has given us, and what he is doing in our lives, through the Spirit. We may wonder why some have apparently been showered with gifts, while others appear less favoured; but our wondering should be redirected to our gifts, and to what God intends us to do with them. These gifts have not been bestowed purely for our benefit, but for us to use in the service of others.

Recognizing the talents we have been given, and then being open to God in the employing of them, is a recipe for exciting living: it is not a quick solution to all our problems, for God has given us a lifetime to work out what he has worked in.

৵

Proper 1 YEAR B

Isa. 40.21–31; Ps. 147.1–11, 20; 1 Cor. 9.16–23; Mark 1.29–39

PROCLAIMING THE MESSAGE

From the epistle: 'If I proclaim the gospel, this gives me no ground for boasting, for an obligation is laid on me, and woe to me if I do not proclaim the gospel!' (1 Cor. 9.16)

For Paul, proclaiming the message was paramount. He told Timothy: 'Proclaim the message; be persistent whether the time is favourable or unfavourable ... do the work of an evangelist, carry out your ministry fully' (2 Tim. 4.2, 5). There is no unfavourable time where the gospel is concerned – and the response of those with whom it is shared is not our business, but God's. Provided we have done our part, we can leave the rest to him.

The gospel never wearies with the telling: new every morning come insights and applications, for each and every situation. When we have grown tired of the message, we are tired of life itself. Can we reflect on the situations in which Paul preached, and bring something of his fervour, compulsion and urgency into our own ministry? Paul did not need a clerical collar: the obligation of proclaiming the message is on every Christian.

☙

Proper 1 YEAR C

Isa. 6.1–8[9–13]; Ps. 138; 1 Cor. 15.1–11; Luke 5.1–11

CATCHING PEOPLE

From the gospel: 'Then Jesus said to Simon, "Do not be afraid; from now on you will be catching people." ' (Luke 5.10b)

Before Jesus had come on the scene, Simon and his friends had been professional fishermen, able to support themselves and their families by expertise in Galilee's waters. Then God intervened, and their sudden inability to net even one fish until Jesus had taken command left the men in no doubt that the time had come to ally themselves with this new Master. Their previous ability would not be wasted: instead, it would be channelled into a far more exciting and fulfilling employment.

We may have followed a particular job or vocation for many years, only to find that suddenly (or perhaps gradually) the skills we thought we had honed pretty well are now either obsolete or are not producing the results on which we have been relying. Is it time for a sea-change, a change for greater work for God? Peter and the other disciples would not find any fault in themselves to account for their night's fishing fiasco. If we are similarly placed, what is God telling us, or asking us, to do?

Deut. 30.15–20 or Ecclus. 15.15–20; Ps. 119.1–8; 1 Cor. 3.1–9; Matt. 5.21–37

OUR CHOICE

From the apocrypha: 'If you choose, you can keep the commandments, and to act faithfully is a matter of your own choice ... He has not commanded anyone to be wicked, and he has not given anyone permission to sin.' (Ecclus. 15.15, 20)

Thank God, we are not automatons! We can share tears and joy; we can endeavour great things; we can make mistakes, and recover from them. We can *live*! Every minute of our lives, we exercise God's most daring and challenging gift of free will. Do we become more proficient as time goes by? Perhaps God alone knows how far round the bend we are on our learning curve!

We choose our way. Ben Sira, however, presents a very Jewish standpoint, in making no mention of any divine grace by which we can reach out and take the right path. Yet in v. 20 he underlines the truth that sin's existence is not due to God. This was built upon later by James (Jas. 1.13); but a number of rabbinical texts took a different line, e.g. 'I created the evil *yetzer* (tendency), I created for him (mankind) the law as a means of healing. If you occupy yourselves with the law, you will not fall into the power of it' (TB *Qxiddushin*, 30b; see also Midrash *Bereshith Rabba*, XXVII).

∂

Proper 2   YEAR B

2 Kings 5.1–14; Ps. 30; 1 Cor. 9.24–27; Mark 1.40–45

VIP TREATMENT?

From the prophets: 'But Naaman became angry and went away, saying, "I thought that for me he would surely come out, and stand and call on the name of the LORD his God, and would wave his hand over the spot, and cure the leprosy!" ' (2 Kings 5.11)

Isn't it sad when we are not treated with the respect we deserve! But how generous are *we* in affirming others? Their dignity matters more than ours, but ours will be saved if we put theirs first. Paul is keen to emphasize that the elevated position carries risks all its own; and yet there is an added incentive in the realization that every effort on the part of those in positions of prominence will certainly not go unnoticed.

We may get the balance wrong, through innocence. The leper whom Jesus had healed was unable to keep the news secret; and although his impulsiveness may have curtailed Jesus' ministry in the short term (Mark 1.45), it led to more people making more effort to obtain healing. Naaman's recalcitrance led to faith in Elisha being openly expressed by his servants – and who knows where this led?

Whenever we feel tempted to wallow in affronted dignity, let's be quick to share something good with those nearest to us. It may make an awesome difference to someone's life – besides our own.

ॐ

Proper 2 YEAR C

Jer. 17.5–10; Ps. 1; 1 Cor. 15.12–20; Luke 6.17–26

HOLISTIC MINISTRY

From the gospel: 'They had come to hear him and to be healed of their diseases; and those who were troubled with unclean spirits were cured.' (Luke 6.18)

Jesus provided a threefold ministry: to the mind, body and soul. Teaching, healing and spiritual cleansing. He was not only concerned to improve the quality of life for the hereafter, but also for the present. The Church needs to practise this same tripartite ministry, in a world more densely populated than ever before.

How are we doing? Preaching the word, sharing the gospel, exercising a ministry of healing for the body and the spirit – in every church, among every congregation? The challenge is immense: perhaps we are doing what we can, but perhaps we could do more.

What are people looking to the Church for today? For comfort, reassurance, stimulation, excitement, knowledge, healing, truth, faith? And more! And if we do not help these people, they will go elsewhere. Let us pray for guidance to meet their needs, rejoicing that the gaining of each person sets the angelic choirs alight with praise (Luke 15.10)!

Lev. 19.1–2, 9–18; Ps. 119.33–40; 1 Cor. 3.10–11, 16–23; Matt. 5.38–48

LOVE'S FOUNDATION

From the epistle: 'For no one can lay any foundation other than the one that has been laid; that foundation is Jesus Christ.' (1 Cor. 3.11)

Jesus undergirds everything we do and say and are in his name. The foundations of a building do not become obsolete as each storey is completed: rather, they become more important as more stress is laid on them. As we press forward in faith, God intends that we should rely ever more on our Saviour. A child does not evaluate the extent of its dependence on others: it is only when maturity comes that we realize our need, and can appreciate it accordingly.

The hard work has already been done for us. We may have been capable of undergoing crucifixion; but no one but Christ could have completed the Church's foundation, by powering through hell, dispossessing Satan of his keys and power, and restoring life where death had been.

When we realize that such power underlies the love we extend in Jesus' name, we can do and say and be someone greater than ourselves: we are not on our own; we are not our own.

☙

Proper 3   YEAR B

Isa. 43.18–25; Ps. 41; 2 Cor. 1.18–22; Mark 2.1–12

FIRST INSTALMENT

From the epistle: 'But it is God who established us with you in Christ and has anointed us, by putting his seal on us and giving us his Spirit in our hearts as a first instalment.' (2 Cor. 1.21–12)

The Dutch evangelist Corrie ten Boom used to recall her father's lesson that, just as a railway ticket is purchased at the station just before one boards the train, so God does not give us grace to complete next week's tasks until the need is actually there. His method of working is this: to plant the Holy Spirit in our hearts as a downpayment, and to make subsequent additions as each task becomes due. Can we not trust him to be faithful?

Thy strength I'll supply,
And thy wages I'll pay.

(Sacred Songs and Solos, no. 4)

Jesus promised that the Spirit would bring God's word to mind (John 14.26): the first instalment of a spiritual fortune that we build on by taking it and sharing it with others, allowing God to give us a rate of interest greater than the Footsie 100 would dare to contemplate.

This is God at his most magnificently unfair.

∂

Proper 3   YEAR C
Gen. 45.3–11, 15; Ps. 37.1–11, 39–40; 1 Cor. 15.35–38, 42–50; Luke 6.27–38

HONEST RETURN

From the gospel: 'Give, and it will be given to you. A good measure, pressed down, shaken together, running over, will be put into your lap; for the measure you give will be the measure you get back.' (Luke 6.38)

Around the time of Jesus, there were two rival prestigious rabbinical schools in Jerusalem: one headed by the austere, hard-line Rabbi Shammai; the other by the moderate Rabbi Hillel. A young man challenged Hillel one day: 'You'll make a proselyte of me if you can tell me the whole law while I stand on one leg!' Hillel regarded him steadily, and replied: 'Do not do to your neighbour what you would not do to yourself. That is the whole law. The rest is commentary. Go and learn' (TB *Shabbat*, 31a).

God does not deal with a niggardly hand. If we delight in him and his will, he responds with magnificent unfairness. The world is not so generously reciprocative, but it will generally respond to goodness. Subconsciously, we all need love, respect, recognition and affirmation. You will receive it, says Jesus, in the measure in which you give it.

❖ The Second Sunday Before Lent

Gen. 1.1—2.3; Ps. 136 or Ps. 136.1–9, 23–26; Rom. 8.18–25; Matt. 6.25–34

LIVING IN HOPE

From the epistle: 'For in hope we were saved. Now hope that is seen is not hope. For who hopes for what is seen? But if we hope for what we do not see, we wait for it with patience.' (Rom. 8.24–25).

Three shining examples of hope and patience come to mind: Abraham, who trusted in God's promise of a son for 25 years; Polycarp, Bishop of Smyrna, who refused to recant when faced with martyrdom after 86 years' trust in Christ; and Monica, who prayed for the conversion of her husband for 16 years, and for that of her son for 22 years – her son who was to become known as Augustine of Hippo, saint and doctor of the Church.

This is hopeful, trustful stamina of high degree, stamina to which we all need to aspire. God is no respecter of persons: if he can endow the Abrahams, Polycarps and Monicas of this world with such hope, he can do the same for us.

Patience is not merely an acquiescence that says: I will wait for such and such, and whether it happens or not, I will continue to believe. Patience is more positive: I will wait in hope, that this thing *will* come to pass.

Have you been given a hope? Hang on to it, no matter how improbable it seems. God is a Master of the impossible.

❧

The Second Sunday Before Lent

Prov. 8.1, 22–31; Ps. 104.24–35; Col. 1.15–20; John 1.1–14

JESUS FIRST

From the epistle: 'He is the head of the body, the church; he is the beginning, the firstborn from the dead, so that he might come to have first place in everything.' (Col. 1.18)

He came to his own people, but they would not give him his rightful place. He comes to us – and what welcome do we give him? Do we put anyone or anything before Jesus in our lives?

The dearest idol I have known,
Whate'er that idol be,
Help me to tear it from Thy throne,
And worship only Thee.

   (William Cowper)

With God from the beginning, firstborn in the new life, founder of the Church – Jesus is the first example of everything we know. Can we comprehend this? No, we need simply to take it on trust. He has never taken second place, except in the hearts of those who put Satan first.

We live in a world where compromise is rife. Contracts are drawn up, yet before the ink is dry, loopholes are sought. Statutes are formulated, yet before they have made history, modifications, alterations, additions and caveats have rendered them obsolete.

May we strive to be consistent in giving Jesus first place, whatever the cost.

৯

The Second Sunday Before Lent   YEAR C
Gen. 2.4b–9, 15–25; Ps. 65; Rev. 4; Luke 8.22–25

THE OPEN DOOR

From the epistle: 'After this I looked, and there in heaven a door stood open! And the first voice, which I had heard speaking to me like a trumpet, said, "Come up here, and I will show you what must take place after this." ' (Rev. 4.1)

John has already heard, in the message to the Philadelphian Church: 'I have set before you an open door, which no one is able to shut' (Rev. 3.8). Now he sees an even more important open door: one that opens on to a universal message, from the throne-room of heaven itself.

God opens doors for us throughout our lives: some small, which show us a little more of his purpose; some magnificently large, which, when we enter, change the course of our lives in a major way. Occasionally, we are privileged, like John, to be given a glimpse of heaven; when a great truth dawns, there comes a new insight into a scripture text, a prayer is convincingly answered ... there in heaven a door stood open!

These times cannot be booked in advance – nor, once given, can they be extended to suit our preferences. Peter and the others could not stay on the mountain (Luke 9.33), but neither was the storm prolonged beyond their endurance (Luke 8.24). The opening – and closing – of a door is in the hands of God.

❖ The Sunday Next Before Lent   YEAR A

Exod. 24.12–18; Ps. 2 or Ps. 99; 2 Pet. 1.16–21; Matt. 17.1–9

MOVED BY THE SPIRIT

From the epistle: 'First of all you must understand this, that no prophecy of scripture is a matter of one's own interpretation, because no prophecy ever came by human will, but men and women moved by the Holy Spirit spoke from God.' (2 Pet. 1.20–21)

It is often the case that a carefully prepared and constructed sermon will produce less response from a congregation than one that has had to be delivered without notice, when the scheduled preacher has failed to turn up! This is the Holy Spirit at work, and enjoying it! If we could only 'let go and let God' move in us more often, perhaps more people, more of the time, would respond to this indefinable, yet mighty, power.

Have we ever been moved to respond to a situation, a question, a dilemma, in a way that afterwards surprised us, a way that seemed quite out of character, and yet that turned out for the best? This is the Holy Spirit at work.

He is here within each of us, to be used: yet surely he must be the least-used dynamo the world has yet seen. Can we reflect on the *Shekinah*-glory of the transfiguration, and allow something of its power and presence to activate and motivate a great appreciation of our dynamic Spirit?

ॐ

The Sunday Next Before Lent   YEAR B

2 Kings 2.1–12; Ps. 50.1–6; 2 Cor. 4.3–6; Mark 9.2–9

SERVUS SERVORUM

From the epistle: 'For we do not proclaim ourselves; we proclaim Jesus Christ as Lord and ourselves as your slaves for Jesus' sake.' (2 Cor. 4.5)

To see ourselves as others see us is a desire not confined to Robert Burns; but for others to see Jesus in us is an indication of our Christian commitment to let nothing of ourselves obliterate the Lord whose ambassadors we are.

It is no use looking at others and taking heart from the (doubtful) fact that we are making a better job of our discipleship than they are. Each of us is called to fill a unique rôle, and it is as individuals that we are called and chosen into the great body of Christ, the Church. How do we present Jesus to others? How do we serve other servants of Christ, in his name? How do we subsume our natural inclinations under his virtues?

The natural inclination of the world is to follow its own way, not God's. Therefore, when we present Christian values – the fruit of the Spirit: love, joy, peace, patience, kindness, generosity, faithfulness, gentleness and self-control – we shall, more often than not, be misunderstood. But that is infinitely better than not being recognized as Christians.

꙳

The Sunday Next Before Lent   YEAR C
Exod. 34.29–35; Ps. 99; 2 Cor. 3.12—4.2; Luke 9.28–36[37–43]

TAKE HEART!

From the epistle: 'Therefore, since it is by God's mercy that we are engaged in this ministry, we do not lose heart.' (2 Cor. 4.1)

Moses had been a recalcitrant recruit, putting forward all the reasons he could think of why God should choose someone else to lead the Israelites out of Egypt. Yet God had got his way, and had changed Moses from an undisciplined, impulsive man into a confident, committed leader. God can do the same for us. We have been called and chosen for ministry – lay and ordained. By his mercy, at our calling, we have had his abundant grace and mercy made available: whether or not we avail ourselves of it is up to us.

The conditions are hard: but they are so wonderfully impossible that without God we should have no chance at all. Only by our inner spiritual peace can we remain on duty in a perpetual war zone; only by prayer can we learn our strengths and weaknesses, our limitation and potential.

We are not to lose heart, because to do so would not only be inconsistent with our calling, but would also compromise its culmination.

LENT

❖ **Ash Wednesday**   YEARS A, B, C

Joel 2.1–2, 12–17 or Isa. 58.1–12; Ps. 51.1–17; 2 Cor. 5.20b—6.10; Matt.
6.1–6, 16–21 or John 8.1–11

A WILLING SPIRIT

From the psalter: 'Create in me a clean heart, O God, and put a new and
right spirit within me. Do not cast me away from your presence, and do
not take your holy spirit from me. Restore to me the joy of your
salvation, and sustain in me a willing spirit.' (Ps. 51.10–12)

These verses, if not the whole of the Miserere, can profitably be taken as
our daily prayer for Lent. We may retire into a wilderness – of our own
making, or another's – but we are still in God's presence. Lent is a time
for reflection rather than morbid self-examination; for a revitalizing of
the joy to be found in simply knowing God; and for a rekindling of
willingness to serve him.

Can we work on these during Lent? Can we reflect on who we are,
why we are where we are, and how we can best show Christ to the world
where we are? A tall order! But the next six and a half weeks will prepare
us for new life in the Easter joy. Lent is a time for renewal, even as
nature is preparing to resume growth after the winter. Let us not dwell
so much on what can be given up in Lent, as on what can be taken on
board and shared with others.

If we can be strengthened with the joy of our Lord (Neh. 8.10), and
a willingness to be totally committed to his message, it will give Lent a
whole new meaning to those around us.

❖ **The First Sunday of Lent**   YEAR A

Gen. 2.15–17; 3.1–7; Ps. 32; Rom. 5.12–19; Matt. 4.1–11

'AWAY WITH YOU, SATAN!'

From the gospel: 'Jesus said to him, "Away with you, Satan! For it is
written, 'Worship the Lord your God, and serve only him'." Then the

devil left him, and suddenly angels came and waited on him.' (Matt. 4.10–11)

We can emulate Jesus, and prepare our arsenal so that every time Satan attacks us we have a scriptural defence. Each of us has far more of the Bible already in our memory than we think: and we shall probably not be at the famished end of a 40-day fast when our temptation rolls up.

Today, with more versions of the Bible than ever before, it is not difficult to find the one that suits us best. Let us set aside even a small portion of each day this Lent for quiet reading, reflection and memorizing of these passages, building our scriptural tower of defence against the time of Satan's onslaught.

There are over 7,000 promises in the Bible. When we have committed even half of those to memory, the practice will have become a habit!

Dr Billy Graham once said: 'Fifteen minutes alone with God at the start of every day can change situations and remove mountains.' Let us put it to the test this Lent.

⤚

The First Sunday of Lent YEAR B

Gen. 9.8–17; Ps. 25.1–10; 1 Pet. 3.18–22; Mark 1.9–15

SPIRIT-DRIVEN

From the gospel: 'And the Spirit immediately drove him out into the wilderness. He was in the wilderness forty days, tempted by Satan; and he was with the wild beasts; and the angels waited on him.' (Mark 1.12–13)

Of the three Gospel accounts of Jesus' temptations, perhaps Mark's is the earliest. It is certainly the most daring, in suggesting that Jesus did not go of his own volition into the dreary, barren place of testing. It also shows the great power of the Holy Spirit; if it could take over the will of Jesus so convincingly, what can it do in our lives? Perhaps the Spirit is already having its way with us.

Has God led you into a wilderness? Is your life at present dark and dreary? Are others preying on your weakness, your inability to retaliate? Have circumstances pressed in upon you, until you do not know where to turn? Take the problem to Jesus: explain it in all the detail you can, and trust him to do what is necessary. But note that while Mark implies the angels were ministering to Jesus from the start, Matthew (Matt. 4.11) has them appearing after the temptations; and Luke (Luke 4.1–13) does not mention them at all. We cannot rely on God following a precise pattern in our lives; he will not be so constricted. But he has promised that we shall not be tested beyond our limits (1 Cor. 10.13).

❧

The First Sunday of Lent YEAR C

Deut. 26.1–11; Ps. 91.1–2, 9–16; Rom 10.8b–13; Luke 4.1–13[14] (verse 14 is in addition to the lectionary!)

SPIRIT-FILLED

From the gospel: 'Jesus, full of the Holy Spirit, returned from the Jordan and was led by the Spirit in the wilderness, . . . Then Jesus, filled with the power of the Spirit, returned to Galilee.' (Luke 4.1, 14a)

The ordeal of Satan's temptatious had not diminished the power of the Spirit in Jesus one iota! Filled to the brim at the outset, he had exactly the same complete spiritual composition even after Satan had done his worst. In his three-year ministry, being limited in a physical body, Jesus was to experience physical tiredness and exhaustion; but there was nothing in the natural or the spiritual world that could touch his spiritual stamina.

We may marvel at this – but, after all, Jesus is the Son of God. Yet there is something even more surprising: Jesus tells us we shall do 'greater works' than those he worked (John 14.12), because we shall not only be Spirit-filled but, with our spiritual reservoirs topped up to overflowing, in the victory of Calvary.

Satan's present-day onslaughts can, therefore, be met not only blow for blow, but can be overcome by a magnificently unfair margin if God is having his way with us.

❖ The Second Sunday of Lent YEAR A

Gen. 12.1–4a; Ps. 121; Rom. 4.1–5, 13–17; John 3.1–17

SENT TO SAVE

From the gospel: 'Indeed, God did not send the Son into the world to condemn the world, but in order that the world might be saved through him.' (John 3.17)

Jesus came to give the world a chance; but the day of his visitation ended, and many had thrown their chance away. If he were to come back today, it would probably be the same. What does it take to persuade people to believe, if a resurrection does not manage it?

'Not by might, nor by power, but by my Spirit,' God still says. There is no compulsion, no necessity to believe; and there lies the mystery. Nicodemus could not grasp the mystery of rebirth, don though he was. We may wonder at a man of intellect being so obtuse, while simple fishermen believed. Yet God has given us muscular brains: we are not to despise intellect, but to use it discerningly, sifting, testing, weighing information and data, examining whether it is of God or not; and discarding anything that conflicts with the Christian creed.

Jesus did not condemn those who did not believe: he wept over them. For it is not in God's nature to wish destruction on any. How often do we weep for others?

❧

The Second Sunday of Lent YEAR B

Gen. 17.1–7, 15–16; Ps. 22.23–31; Rom. 4.13–25; Mark 8.31–38

FULLY CONVINCED

From the epistle: 'No distrust made him waver concerning the promise of God, but he grew strong in his faith as he gave glory to God, being fully convinced that God was able to do what he had promised.' (Rom. 4.20–21)

For 25 years Abraham kept faith with God. People would mock at an old man calling himself 'Father of Many Nations'. Sarah would doubtless fret and despair. But Abraham did not waver; and probably once Isaac had been born, the quarter-century did not seem so long in retrospect.

Paul is obviously impressed with the fact that not only did Abraham remain loyal, but his faith also strengthened during that waiting period: it grew, until it welled up in a mighty surge of confidence – and Isaac was born. May we also increase our faith, in *hopes* of the fulfilment of our prayers, instead of waiting *until* those prayers are answered.

'Pray to God, sailor, but row for the shore.' The rabbis phrased it thus: 'Pray and pray, again and again; a time will come when you will be answered' (Midrash *Debarim Rabba*, 3.24).

God responds to a firm conviction on the part of the pray-er. Are we listening?

❧

The Second Sunday of Lent · YEAR C
Gen. 15.1–12, 17–18; Ps. 27; Phil. 3.17—4.1; Luke 13.31–35

EXPECTING A SAVIOUR

From the epistle: 'But our citizenship is in heaven, and it is from there that we are expecting a Saviour, the Lord Jesus Christ. He will transform the body of our humiliation that it may be conformed to the body of his glory, by the power that also enables him to make all things subject to himself.' (Phil. 3.20–21)

An old painting is discovered, probably in an attic full of cobwebs. It is lovingly and painstakingly restored, and people exclaim: 'What a transformation!', marvelling at the colours and details that have been brought to light. So it will be at the Coming of Christ, promises Paul, looking ahead in eager expectation. The physical body, with its limitation of our inherently beautiful spiritual nature, will become something glorious: quite how, no one but God knows!

So enthralled with the glorious prospect, the early Church was convinced of a fairly immediate parousia. When it delayed, the Christians marshalled all they could recall of the promises and teaching of Jesus, and realized that God's timing is very different from ours – and that worldwide evangelism must precede Christ's Second Coming. The Church is still working on it. Where are we in this great schedule?

❖ The Third Sunday of Lent YEAR A

Exod. 17.1–7; Ps. 95; Rom 5.1–11; John 4.5–42

FAITH COMES BY HEARING

From the gospel: 'Many Samaritans from that city believed in him because of the woman's testimony, ... And many more believed because of his word. They said to the woman, "It is no longer because of what you said that we believe, for we have heard for ourselves, and we know that this is truly the Saviour of the world."' (John 4.39, 41–42)

Probably most of us come to faith by hearing another's testimony. It's a good beginning, but consolidation only comes when we listen to Christ himself. Even the devil knows about Jesus: we need to know Christ, one to one, before we can affirm: 'This is truly the Saviour of the world' - *and of me.* 'Whom do other people say Jesus is?' is a nice theological exercise. But when he comes close and asks us directly: 'Whom do *you* say I am', the time for real commitment and integrity has come: we have reached the stage where hearing matures into faith, and faith declares: 'Lord, I'm ready to do what you want, go where you will, and be what you intend me to be.'

Have we reached this stage? How much of our attention has Jesus got? If he has brought us this far, he will not let us go. He will have his way with us. We have passed the vital point of no return.

≈

The Third Sunday of Lent YEAR B

Exod. 20.1–17; Ps. 19; 1 Cor 1.18–25; John 2.13–22

PROPHECY FULFILLED

From the gospel: 'After he was raised from the dead, his disciples remembered that he had said this; and they believed the scripture and the word that Jesus had spoken.' (John 2.22)

Prophecy continues to be spoken, and fulfilled. Doubtless God has an overall pattern, but we merely see in the Bible many very different prophecies – some coming to pass earlier, some later, and many still not fulfilled. In its day, the decalogue covered every aspect of the Jews' life and worship. Then Jesus came with a 'new commandment' – but still he approved of the Mosaic laws (Luke 18.20), which he had not come to destroy, but to fulfil.

Many of the first-century Jews did not get the balance right between knowing what in Jesus was being fulfilled, and what he was introducing as the new way to follow. To a lesser degree, we have a balance to strike today: what from the past is too precious to discard, and what in the present is too vital to ignore? The Church is not a child condemned to an eternal kindergarten; nor is it an orphan destitute of family and background: the old landmarks are essential for navigation today, while our present generation will be expected to give those to come spiritual directions for the future. Each of us has a part to play in fulfilling yesterday's prophecy, and in writing tomorrow's.

✢

The Third Sunday of Lent   YEAR C

Isa. 55.1–9; Ps. 63.1–8; 1 Cor. 10.1–13; Luke 13.1–9

MERCIFUL PROVISION

From the epistle: 'No testing has overtaken you that is not common to everyone. God is faithful, and he will not let you be tested beyond your strength, but with the testing he will also provide the way out so that you may be able to endure it.' (1 Cor. 10.13)

Vineyards are designed for grape harvests. The fig tree in Jesus' parable had been a later introduction, but it still merited care and attention. If it responded well, its place in the vineyard would be honoured. So we, as Gentiles, have been introductions to the Jewish vineyard. We shall be tested, but if we do well, we shall occupy places of honour among the vines: God's growing things, on God's ground, in God's sight.

We may expect the same attention from our Gardener as the vines already there from the vineyard's first planting have received. All – early or late introductions – will be culled if growth and yield fall below par. Our pruning and training will be rigorous, but mercifully tailored to our individual strengths and weaknesses. Thus, like Paul, can we not 'give thanks in all circumstances'? (1 Thess. 5.18.) Can we have the grace to realize that the sharper the pruning, the greater the harvest? Only the most promising vines – and figs – are trained.

❖ The Fourth Sunday of Lent YEARS A, B, C
(Mothering Sunday)

Exod. 2.1–10 or 1 Sam 1.20–28; Ps. 34.11–20 or Ps. 127.1–4; 2 Cor. 1.3–7 or Col. 3.12–17; Luke 2.33–35 or John 19.25–27

A MOTHER'S LOVE

From the gospel: 'Then Simeon blessed them and said to his mother Mary, "This child is destined for the falling and the rising of many in Israel, and to be a sign that will be opposed so that the inner thoughts of many will be revealed – and a sword will pierce your own soul too."' (Luke 2.34–35)

Being a mother is not easy, whether the mother in question is of an ordinary family, or of the world's Saviour, or – as Holy Mother Church – of millions of Christians in this world and the next. Today's mothers, at least, follow in a centuries-old line of mothers. Yet Mary had no example to follow as, daily under God's guidance, she learned how to be the mother of God himself. Hers was a testing without precedent: 'Maiden yet a Mother, Daughter of thy Son' (Dante Alighieri, 1285–1321, tr. R. A. Knox).

Remember also Monica, mentioned earlier, who prayed for 22 years for the conversion of her son. Her perseverance and love was rewarded in the legacy that Augustine (of Hippo) left to the Church. Remember also the mother of James and John, risking reputation and dignity for her sons (Matt. 20.20); and the love and regard for Mary that Jesus, in direst agony, showed at Calvary (John 19.26).

> Shall we not love thee, Mother dear,
> Whom Jesus loved so well?
>
> (Henry Williams Baker, 1821–77)

❖ The Fifth Sunday of Lent YEAR A
(Passiontide begins)

Ezek. 37.1–14; Ps. 130; Rom. 8.6–11; John 11.1–45

RESTORATION

From the prophets: '"I will put my spirit within you, and you shall live, and I will place you on your own soil; then you shall know that I, the LORD, have spoken and will act," says the LORD.' (Ezek. 37.14)

In the vision of the Valley of Dry Bones in the Old Testament, Ezekiel was given courage to look forward to Israel's return from exile. With restoration would come testing, but there would be strength to meet it. In the New Testament, Lazarus was given a new lease of life, but this too would bring danger (John 12.10). The Holy Spirit's indwelling brings both short-term strength and eternal life: who can deny that we are infinitely more blessed than Ezekiel or Lazarus?

On this Passion Sunday we reflect on the agony this gift of the Spirit cost our Lord. The realization of what he was making available to us saw Jesus through the trauma (Heb. 12.2). Can we imagine what our plight would have been had we still been condemned to paying the penalty for Adam's fall? We should have had no soil to call our own – here, or Hereafter.

෭

The Fifth Sunday of Lent YEAR B
(Passiontide begins)

Jer. 31.31–34; Ps. 51.1–12 or Ps. 119.9–16; Heb. 5.5–10; John 12.20–33

FOR THIS REASON

From the gospel: 'Now my soul is troubled. And what should I say – "Father, save me from this hour"? No, it is for this reason that I have come to this hour.' (John 12.27)

Jesus was not going to renege on his mission, but he was troubled, and he did not mind his closest friends sharing his anguish. It may be from the best of reasons that we soldier on alone in stoical silence, but we are truly blessed if we have friends with whom we can share trouble as well as joy.

Our Lord could have operated his three-year ministry as a solo act; but from the outset he chose to involve people from a variety of backgrounds, whom he generously – and genuinely – called 'friends' (John 15.15), and with whom he was lovingly patient and loyal. When he sent them out to preach, it was in pairs (Mark 6.7).

But in Gethsemane, and at Calvary, they left him, their faith so shattered that by Easter morning he had difficulty in persuading them that the unbelievable had really happened.

For what reason are we living today? And is it a reason that includes our friends or not?

❦

The Fifth Sunday of Lent
(Passiontide begins)

Isa. 43.16–21; Ps. 126; Phil. 3.4b–14; John 12.1–8

WANTING TO KNOW

From the epistle: 'I want to know Christ and the power of his resurrection and the sharing of his sufferings by becoming like him in his death, if somehow I may attain the resurrection from the dead.' (Phil. 3.10)

Can we come to know Christ with Paul's fervour? Today's world in general is incapable of wonder, of awe, of excitement, where the things of God are concerned. Can we go so far down the road of faith that we cannot get back? If it were to be made a crime to be a Christian, would we be acquitted for lack of evidence?

Becoming like Jesus in his death means we are impervious to the world's allure, and constantly on 'red alert' against Satan. We have passed the point of no return, and there is nothing holding us back. When Mary broke the seal on her perfume, the roomful of guests was alerted. However confused she may have felt, there was no way the jar could be resealed: her work – and her love – for Jesus had to go ahead.

Let us not be afraid of casting the die for God. Every day he will bring us to the point of decision. We either choose his way – or someone else's.

❖ Palm Sunday
(Liturgy of the Passion)

Isa. 50.4–9a; Ps. 31.9–16; Phil. 2.5–11; Matt. 26.14—27.66 or Matt. 27.11–54

STAY WITH ME

From the gospel: 'He took with him Peter and the two sons of Zebedee, and began to be grieved and agitated. Then he said to them, "I am

deeply grieved, even to death; remain here, and stay awake with me." '
(Matt. 26.37–8)

Often in our lowest moments, all we want to do is to be alone; but Jesus
put a higher value on friendship. After the resurrection, his disciples
would remember this, and in turn would be encouraged to share more
of their lives with others: to rejoice with the joyful, and to weep with the
sorrowing.

'Being alongside' is the key to showing love and concern in so many
ways, often when words would be difficult or unnecessary. We may think
we have no time to spare, yet time shared with those in need is time saved
for God. If we put his business first, he will see that we have time enough.

The anguish of Jesus in Gethsemane was compounded by his ability
to know the future. He could see those whom he had come to save
plotting his death; that their machinations would in the end be
unsuccessful did not remove the sting of their treachery.

And we too were on his mind. May he be on ours today.

❧

Palm Sunday   YEAR B
(Liturgy of the Passion)

Isa. 50.4–9a; Ps. 31.9–16; Phil 2.5–11; Mark 14.1—15.47 or Mark 15.1–39
[40–47]

BETRAYED

From the gospel: 'Now the betrayer had given them a sign, saying, "The
one I will kiss is the man; arrest him and lead him away under guard." '
(Mark 14.44)

Surely the guard was against any who might try to rescue Jesus? Did not
Judas know Jesus himself would never use violence? Or had he been
with Christ for three years, and yet – like Philip – apparently still did not
know him? (John 14.9.)

We also may have been with Jesus a long time, but today can we
reflect on how well we know him? Do we still try to bargain with him, to
promise certain things provided he will do his part? Do we ask for proof,
while he is asking simply for faith? Whatever Judas' motives were, he was
awry in his calculations. Yet he had once been so close to Jesus.

How often had he kissed his Lord, before Gethsemane? Perhaps we would not be so base in our betrayal – but let us resolve to watch the *little* discrepancies: the undercharging we do not report; the unfranked stamp we use again; the speed limit we exceed. Even Judas' downward path had to have a first step somewhere back along the line.

ॐ

Palm Sunday YEAR C
(Liturgy of the Passion)

Isa. 50.4–9a; Ps. 31.9–16; Phil. 2.5–11; Luke 22.14—23.56 or Luke 23.1–49

SIFTED AS WHEAT

From the gospel: 'Simon, Simon, listen! Satan has demanded to sift all of you like wheat, but I have prayed for you that your own faith may not fail; and you, when once you have turned back, strengthen your brothers.' (Luke 22.31–32)

Jesus knew that his closest friend would break down and cry bitter tears before the night was over; strong man though he was, Satan would have his way with him. But there would be a turning back from denial, and when once Peter had reached that turning, he would be able to help others in similar situations.

Until we have experienced grief, trauma, loss, doubt, fear, we cannot truly help those so afflicted; we may have some idea of what they are going through, but we cannot say: 'I've been there, too!'

The ministry of strengthening is vital, for young and mature Christians alike: all need an on-going affirmation in their vocation. Jesus had been strengthening his disciples for three years, gently leading them on, to new and bigger things. Let us pledge ourselves to do the same, praying for guidance as to when to press forward and when to take a rest. Heaven has never been reached in a single bound.

❖ Monday of Holy Week YEARS A, B, C
Isa. 42.1–9; Ps. 36.5–11; Heb. 9.11–15; John 12.1–11

CONTINUING POVERTY

From the gospel: 'Jesus said, "Leave her alone. She bought it so that she might keep it for the day of my burial. You always have the poor with you, but you do not always have me."' (John 12.7–8)

It is perhaps strange that Jesus did not hold out any prospect of an end to poverty, though he spent much time curing sickness and disease. Does this mean that God is not interested in alleviating poverty? Surely not. God is able to supply our every need, abundantly. Why, then, did Jesus speak as though poverty was an integral part of life?

The answer lies in trust: if we trust in currency that is not God's, it is like filling a bag with holes. But if we can be reckless enough to put God first, and to trust him for food, clothes and the rest, he will honour that trust. Riches are not bad in themselves; they only become a millstone when we elevate them above the things of God.

And it is not only the affluent who trust in wealth: often the poor are so obsessed with money, or the lack of it, that fear prevents them from shifting their attention off their poverty and on to God.

We can give money to the poor – but this only solves part of the problem: more important than anything we give *to* them is what we give *them*.

❖ Tuesday of Holy Week   YEARS A, B, C

Isa. 49.1–7; Ps. 71.1–14; 1 Cor. 1.18–31; John 12.20–36

WHY ARE WE CALLED?

From the epistle: 'Consider your own call, brothers and sisters: not many of you were wise by human standards, not many were powerful, not many were of noble birth.' (1 Cor. 1.26)

Have you ever wondered why God called you? God does not have to give reasons – which is perhaps just as well if no reason seems to present itself! Paul does not hand out any compliments in this verse; the Corinthians need to realize that they are the recipients of God's grace, which cannot be bought. We, like them, have had nothing to do with our call. God chose us for his purpose, not for the excellence of our CV, or our references, and certainly not for our family tree, distinguished or otherwise, nor for any other merit of ours. We cannot buy, ingratiate, study or talk ourselves into God's grace.

He sees our spiritual potential – which is probably greater by far than we can imagine; and his love and strength take up the challenge of moulding and training us to realize that potential.

It may take a lifetime.
But God will get his way.

❖ Wednesday of Holy Week   YEARS A, B, C

Isa. 50.4–9a; Ps. 70; Heb. 12.1–3; John 13.21–32

THE LORD'S WORD

From the prophets: 'The Lord GOD has given me the tongue of a teacher, that I may know how to sustain the weary with a word. Morning by morning he wakens – wakens my ear to listen as those who are taught.' (Isa. 50.4)

Jesus came to a war-weary, sin-chastened world, where nations were being overrun and strange languages and customs were being forced on people to the detriment of traditions and values that had been cherished for centuries. Hasn't this also a very modern ring?

As he ate with the disciples in the cenacle, and told Judas to 'do quickly' what was in the betrayer's mind (John 13.27); he knew that the hour had come for Jerusalem, and for the world. Only with hindsight would men realize the poignancy of that night. He alone could see it then.

In himself was the sustenance for this weary world, but such was the arrogance and ignorance of people that only a fraction of God's strength was being accepted. How much do we accept today? The more we rely on God, the more of God we have to share with others. Only by letting go of our own desires, our self-sufficiency, our wonderful capacity to see ourselves as the centre of our little world, can we hear and receive God's sustaining word, morning by morning.

❖ Maundy Thursday   YEARS A, B, C

Exod. 12.1–4[5–10], 11–14; Ps. 116.1–2, 12–19; 1 Cor. 11.23–26; John 13.1–17, 31b–35

PROCLAMATION OF DEATH

From the epistle: 'This cup is the new covenant in my blood. Do this, as often as you drink it, in remembrance of me. For as often as you eat this

bread and drink the cup, you proclaim the Lord's death until he comes.'
(1 Cor. 11.25b–26)

In Holy Week the agony of Jesus' death is uppermost; by Sunday, it will
be overlaid by triumph and joy; and, to some degree, this is mirrored in
every human bereavement. We weep when death takes a loved one, yet
in our present-day funeral services the element of thanksgiving is now
much stronger than even 30 years ago. We grieve, but we are
encouraged to 'miss for a little, but not too long; miss them, but let
them go'.

To those outside the Church, our frequent remembrances of Jesus'
death in the Eucharist can seem morbidly introspective. And when non-
believers ask us to explain, what do we say? Very few sermons are
preached simply on this remembrance – because it is anything but
simple. We are proclaiming a death that is Life itself; an agony that is the
greatest triumph the world has ever seen; a Man who is God; a covenant
that is so different from an earthly 'last will and testament'; an ending
that is a beginning. How *can* we explain it?

With a tiny wafer, a chalice of wine – and faith.

❖ Good Friday

YEARS A, B, C
Isa. 52.13—53.12; Ps. 22; Heb. 10.16–25 or Heb. 4.14–16; 5.7–9; John
18.1—19.42

LIFTED HIGH

From the prophets: 'See, my servant shall prosper; he shall be exalted and
lifted up, and shall be very high. Just as there were many who were
astonished at him ... so he shall startle many nations.' (Isa. 52.13–14a,
15a)

However we see Jesus on that first Good Friday, we would hardly
describe him as 'prospering' – even with hindsight. Yet he could
promise 'Paradise' to the penitent thief before the day was over.
Unseen by mortal eye, he would triumph over the 'principalities and
powers' ranged against him in hell, and would dispossess Satan of his
keys of death.

But we see the human weakness, the blood and the torture. We see
him lifted high on the cross, and misunderstood, maligned and mocked

by those he had come to save. And every time sin has been manifested since, a new nail has been driven in, and another tear has been shed. How much more can God take? How can we fathom the love that still cries out to startle many nations back to the straight and narrow?

Saints such as Francis of Assisi, godly men and women such as Padre Pio and Veronica Giuliani, have received the stigmata. Our own hands and feet may not show such wounds – but may this Good Friday not pass before we have let Jesus startle us into renewed fervour to grow in his service, as a token of our gratitude for all he suffered.

❖ **Easter Eve**   YEARS A, B, C
(Other than the Easter Vigil)

Job 14.1–14 or Lam. 3.1–9, 19–24; Ps. 31.1–4, 15–16; 1 Pet. 4.1–8; Matt. 27.57–66 or John 19.38–42

CHRIST-LIKE INTENTION

From the epistle: 'Since therefore Christ suffered in the flesh, arm yourselves also with the same intention (for whoever has suffered in the flesh has finished with sin), so as to live for the rest of your earthly life no longer by human desires but by the will of God.' (1 Pet. 4.1–2)

Where are our thoughts concentrated, on this day of hiatus, when Joseph of Arimathea's tomb is sealed to public view, Jerusalem is going about its Passover business, and Christ's disciples are at their lowest ebb? We can only imagine the ferment in the spiritual world as death's power is broken, and the angels rejoice. Easter Eve is full of mystery: the day of all days when the human side of existence merely waits in the darkness of unknowing.

It is a day for renewed commitment on our part, a time to give to God in earnest of our intention to 'love him more dearly and follow him more nearly, day by day' – in return for the love that gave Jesus to die. Whatever we are doing for him, we can do more; however we are loving him, we can love him more. Yes, we can!

The Jesus of the cross does not meet us today – nor, as yet, does the Jesus of Easter morning. On Easter Eve we are simply face to face with the mystery of the sealed tomb. Let us reach out through that mystery to the very heart of God. Lord, I give you my will today – and my earnest intention to . . .

❖ Easter Vigil

Gen. 1.1—22.4a; Exod. 14.10–31; 15.20–1; Isa. 55.1–11; Ps. 136.1–9, 23–6; Ps. 114; Rom. 6.3–11; Matt. 28.1–10

SUCCESS!

From the prophets: 'For as the rain and the snow come down from heaven, ... so shall my word be that goes out from my mouth; it shall not return to me empty, but it shall accomplish that which I purpose, and succeed in the thing for which I sent it.' (Isa. 55.10a, 11)

Easter is all about successful accomplishment: Jesus has done what he came to do. Yet in all the joy and wonder, the flowers and fine music, we can easily lose sight of the pains he had to go to in order to persuade even his closest friends that success had really triumphed! He could have risen with such power as to shake the whole earth: but where then would have been the need for the faith to believe? Only those with open hearts are going to make anything at all of Easter. God wanted it this way.

Jesus was destined to succeed in his mission: just as rain and snow cannot fall upwards, so it was unthinkable that he would fail in his purpose. Can we not marvel today at the sheer dependability of God? Can we not believe that once he has given us his love, he is determined to do all he can to see us through our mission?

And God can do an awesome work. Today is an earnest of his intention.

❧

Easter Vigil

YEAR B

Gen. 7.1–5, 11–18; 8.6–18; 9.8–13; Exod. 14.10–31; 15.20–1; Ezek. 37.1–14; Ps. 46; Ps. 114; Rom. 6.3–11; Mark 16.1–8

DEAD TO SIN

From the epistle: 'We know that Christ, being raised from the dead, will never die again; death no longer has dominion over him. The death he died, he died to sin, once for all; but the life he lives, he lives to God. So you must consider yourselves dead to sin and alive to God in Christ Jesus.' (Rom. 6.9–11)

Jesus did not rise on Easter morning to bring us a completely new life after we have ended our days on earth: we *must*, says Paul, consider ourselves part of this new life *now*, from the time we commit ourselves to Christ. We are infused with his Spirit, enlivened by his resurrection power.

But how will the world know, unless we show it we are dead to sin and alive with new life? We must demonstrate it in some way for otherwise we are being inconsistent; we are negating the very reason we celebrate today.

'Dead to sin' means that sin no longer attracts or interests us. We can live without it, in a world that is largely obsessed with sin. We shall be regarded as strange. Do we mind? We shall be ridiculed. Do we care? With the empty tomb being a mute reminder of love in action, what are we saying to God on this joyful Easter Day? Only 'Thank You'?

ॐ

Easter Vigil YEAR C

Gen. 22.1–18; Exod. 14.10–31; 15.20–21; Zeph. 3.14–20; Ps. 16; Ps. 114; Rom. 6.3–11; Luke 24.1–12

REMEMBER!

From the gospel: 'Why do you look for the living among the dead? He is not here, but has risen. Remember how he told you, while he was still in Galilee, that the Son of Man must be handed over to sinners, and be crucified, and on the third day rise again.' (Luke 24.5b–7)

With filofaxes, CD-Roms and innumerable lists and memos, we are retraining our minds *not* to remember data. How is this fitting us for mission here, and Hereafter? God gave us muscular, articulate minds to soak up his truths; yet he knows we have the capacity also to forget – so he gives us his Spirit to recall his word for us (John 14.26): surely we can trust him to do the work better than a CD-Rom?

Remember! Remember how God has worked in your life until now. Remember what he has been telling you – and, if you cannot recall it, ask the Spirit to make it clear. The women at the tomb were looking for reassurance: they received it, wrapped in a startlingly unexpected command: 'Remember!'

What is God reminding us of, this Easter?

EASTER

❖ **Easter Day**   YEAR A

Acts 10.34–43 or Jer. 31.1–6; Ps. 118.1–2, 14–24; Col. 3.1–4; John 20.1–18 or Matt. 28.1–10

GO AND TELL

From the gospel: 'Then Jesus said to them, "Do not be afraid; go and tell my brothers to go to Galilee; there they will see me." ' (Matt. 28.10)

They would not go on a fruitless journey. Jesus would be there, in Galilee. It was a resurrection promise. He meets us today, in our joy, with the same dual purpose: to give us our work, and the promise of his presence. We are not required to do the first without the joy of the second; but we are required to take the step of faith and begin the work in order to meet him. Can we meet this challenge? He kept his word on that first Easter. We need have no fear that he will do any less for us. God may surprise (even startle) us by his methods of working, but every promise he makes, he keeps.

'Go and tell.' How are people to share our Easter joy if we keep it to ourselves? They may not believe us: the first disciples did not initially believe the women. But we are to share the news, none the less. The response from those we tell is not our responsibility, but theirs, provided we have shared the gospel as we should. If the resurrection life is growing in us, we shall not be able to stop ourselves telling others. Shyness and diffidence must not come into the equation: 'Do not be afraid'. Who could fear, except to keep such news under wraps?

☙

Easter Day   YEAR B

Acts 10.34–43 or Isa. 25.6–9; Ps. 118.1–2, 14–24; 1 Cor. 15.1–11; John 20.1–18 or Mark 16.1–8

WITNESSES

From the epistle: 'They put him to death by hanging him on a tree; but God raised him on the third day and allowed him to appear, not to all the people but to us who were chosen by God as witnesses, and who ate and drank with him after he rose from the dead.' (Acts 10.39b–41)

We are here, in his house: chosen and called as witnesses, sharing in his Eucharist. We stand alongside Peter and, like Peter, our lives have seen highs and lows; and, just as Peter shared his witness with the non-Jew Cornelius, so we are to witness to those of other creeds, or none at all. Christ died and rose for all, without exceptions. If Easter means less than this to us, then it means nothing at all.

Peter's description of the resurrection is compelling in its simplicity. He does not try to explain it, but emphasizes that even in his resurrected state Jesus could consume food and drink. This, in a body that could dematerialize and translocate at will, is beyond our ken, and must be accepted in faith.

Forty days of post-resurrection life and shared experiences was more than enough to convince the disciples. We have 2,000 years as a foundation for our conviction. How much longer does the world need?

❧

Easter Day   YEAR C

Acts 10.34–43 or Isa. 65.17–25; Ps. 118.1–2, 14–24; 1 Cor. 15.19–26; John 20.1–18 or Luke 24.1–12

CONTINUITY

From the prophets: 'They shall build houses and inhabit them; they shall plant vineyards and eat their fruit. They shall not build and another inhabit; they shall not plant and another eat; for like the days of a tree shall the days of my people be, and my chosen shall long enjoy the work of their hands.' (Isa. 65.21–22)

In the time to come, to which Christ's resurrection points, there will be a continuity that has so far never been experienced: 'Here we have no lasting city' (Heb. 13.14a). Here we build houses and subsequent generations live in them. We sow the land, and others come after us and reap the harvest of our crops. We fashion tools, clothes and artwork, and others inherit them. Christ's resurrection, with its prospect of eternal life, gives us a hope of living completely in a completely new world.

Continuity was something for which, on that first Easter Day, the disciples were not looking; yet as the resurrection-reality began to percolate through to them, it dawned on them that it was continuity with a difference: Jesus, despite his wounds, was different; he had not brought the human limitations back from hell. He was now free to come and go at will.

This resurrected Jesus is different to know – but surely by now we have had more practice than had the disciples on that Easter morning.

❖ The Second Sunday of Easter   YEAR A

Acts 2.14a, 22–32; Ps. 16; 1 Pet. 1.3–9; John 20.19–31

SO I SEND YOU

From the gospel: 'Jesus said to them again, "Peace be with you. As the Father has sent me, so I send you." ' (John 20.21)

If we were ever in any doubt about our mission, Jesus answers us here. We are sent, as he had been sent. And how was that? He had been sent to bring people the gospel. Isaiah had spelt it out, centuries earlier, 'to bring good news ... to proclaim release ... and recovery of sight ... to let the oppressed go free, to proclaim the year of the Lord's favour' (Luke 4.18–19). Jesus had given his CV publicly at the outset of his mission, and it had been too overwhelming for many to believe.

We are not called merely to sing hymns twice or three times a week in church. God delights in our music-making, but he has work for us to do every day; and just as Jesus demonstrated a holistic approach, so we are called – irrespective of our academic qualifications – to minister spiritual, mental and physical help. How we do this is a matter between ourselves and God, as he gives us opportunities he would give to no one else.

It is certain that we do not fully realize the power that has been given us in the resurrected Jesus. How would our part of the world be altered if we were to begin to realize our spiritual potential as Easter people?

❧

The Second Sunday of Easter

Acts 4.32–35; Ps. 133; 1 John 1.1—2.2; John 20.19–31

WE CAN GO OUT FREE

From the epistle: 'But if anyone does sin, we have an advocate with the Father, Jesus Christ the righteous; and he is the atoning sacrifice for our sins, and not for ours only but also for the sins of the whole world.' (1 John 2.1b–2)

The most ungenerous and ungracious thing we can do is to negate the sacrifice of Christ by continuing to sin. We shall lapse occasionally – that is part and parcel of life ever since Adam fell (Rom. 3.23) – but we are not to let sin become a habit. Our advocate is not a stranger, taking up our case for a fee; he is our best Friend, and he knows us so well that we can hide nothing from him. His legal fees have already been paid; his work on our behalf has already been done; but he is too loving to draw the line under our case, keeping us company instead while we still have some way to go before heaven, home and beauty. How safe we are in his hands!

He has shouldered what we could not – the burden of worldwide sin. Any burden that we bring to him is small by comparison – yet large enough, if carried unforgiven, to stand between us and salvation.

Easter gives us the best hope mankind has ever had, but it does not absolve us from all responsibility.

❧

The Second Sunday of Easter

Acts 5.27–32; Ps. 118.14–29 or Ps. 150; Rev. 1.4–8; John 20.19–31

NOT THE WHOLE TRUTH

From the gospel: 'Now Jesus did many other signs in the presence of his disciples, which are not written in this book. But these are written so that you may come to believe that Jesus is the Messiah, the Son of God, and that through believing you may have life in his name.' (John 20.30–31)

'Coming to believe' is for many a gradual process, as little by little our faith is built up and matures. Daily life, with its revelations and encouragements, fills out the gospel narrative, showing us that God's power is as strong as ever, his interest in us is as keen as when Jesus was on earth, and his promises are as rock-solid as they were when the evangelists were inspired to write.

Yet the Gospels are so short! We long to know what else Jesus did and said, where else he went, who else he met. The disciples, says John, witnessed 'many other signs': were these signs of no relevance to us today? Did anyone else take note of them – and, if so, are there more Gospels waiting to be discovered?

But God in his wisdom has decided that the Scriptures we have are sufficient for faith. We may commit whole Gospels to memory – but such is God's word that even the most familiar verses are capable of giving us new insights, new truths. Until we enter glory, we have not the whole truth.

❖ The Third Sunday of Easter   YEAR A

Acts 2.14a, 36–41; Ps. 116.1–4, 12–19; 1 Pet. 1.17–23; Luke 24.13–35

NEW-BORN

From the epistle: 'You have been born anew, not of perishable but of imperishable seed, through the living and enduring word of God.' (1 Pet. 1.23)

We owe our physical make-up to earthly parents, but at baptism we received a new birth from the ever-living word of God: Jesus himself. Spiritually, we are in him, linked by immutable ties that no one on earth can break.

What does this mean in our daily life? Does it give us a sense of journeying through this world rather than living in it? Does it give us not only a longing for the next life, but a really fervent desire to share the gospel with others so that they too can accept it? Does it daily spur us on to use all the time God gives us, for his work? 'All for Jesus' – if we can bring this prayer to bear on every aspect of our lives, even the smallest work will be transformed into something worthwhile and beautiful for God.

Have we today a friend in need? Certainly we have. Let us extend help, in the name of Jesus. Have we today a problem? We probably have several problems. Let us offer them, in detail, to God, for the attention and application of his living word.

The more we train ourselves, by his grace, to do this, the more his word will go to work in our lives. And people will look at us as they looked at the disciples, and declare: 'These folk have been with Jesus!'

෨

The Third Sunday of Easter　　　　　　　　YEAR B

Acts 3.12–19; Ps. 4; 1 John 3.1–7; Luke 24.36b–48

BE NOT DECEIVED

From the epistle: 'Everyone who commits sin is guilty of lawlessness; . . . Little children, let no one deceive you. Everyone who does what is right is righteous, just as he is righteous.' (1 John 3.4a, 7)

John softens the strictures with a loving 'little children'. We are but human, and we break the law at times: we exceed the speed limit, arrive late for a meeting, tell a 'white' lie. If we are not hardened to sin, God will prick our conscience, and we shall quickly ask for forgiveness. When we do right, what then? Our reward is the knowledge that we are walking in Jesus' footsteps, and there is no better place to be.

It can be very difficult to stand up in a public place and say grace before a meal when no one else has the courage to do so, or to go several miles to the shop to correct an under-payment, or to help extricate someone's car from a muddy ditch when we are dressed up to the nines. But, as James reminds us, if we know what to do, but fail to do it, we are guilty of sin (Jas. 4.17).

Nowadays, advice comes to us from all quarters, and John's warning has never been more apposite: we are not to be deceived. Let us pray for a godly discernment; and once we believe we have it, let us ignore anything that runs counter to it.

෨

The Third Sunday of Easter　　　　　　　　YEAR C

Acts 9.1–6[7–20]; Ps. 30; Rev. 5.11–14; John 21.1–19

WITH FULL VOICE

From the epistle: 'Then I looked, and I heard the voice of many angels surrounding the throne and the living creatures and the elders; they numbered myriads of myriads and thousands of thousands, singing with full voice, "Worthy is the Lamb that was slaughtered to receive power ... and glory and blessing!"' (Rev. 5.11–12)

Can we imagine the volume of music from these massed choirs? Yet this is only one of many instances in the Bible where we are shown that heaven is an exciting, vibrant place full of sound. There is no excuse for us whispering through our religion here, in the belief that Hereafter we shall forever speak in hushed voices. God is not fazed by Christians using the full volume of the lungs he has given them. Easter is a good time for making our faith much more audible!

John's visions in Revelation span time, and beyond: past, present and future. The Lamb (Jesus) will carry his wounds for ever, in mute reminder of the cost of our salvation. When we are tempted to sin, however slightly, can we remember those wounds? Can we remember the heavenly host singing with all its might, in honour of the Lamb who gave his all?

What are we giving in return?

❖ The Fourth Sunday of Easter   YEAR A

Acts 2.42–47; Ps. 23; 1 Pet. 2.19–25; John 10.1–10

WE HAVE BEEN HEALED

From the epistle: 'He himself bore our sins in his body on the cross, so that, free from sins, we might live for righteousness; by his wounds you have been healed.' (1 Pet. 2.24)

There are those who confine this healing to the spiritual, but throughout the Gospels Jesus did not differentiate between spiritual and physical healing: at one point, in fact, he underlined the indissoluble link between the two (Mark 2.8f.), and Matthew quotes Isaiah: 'He took our infirmities and bore our diseases' (Matt. 8.17). Freed from the spiritual weight of inherited sin, and the restrictions of illness and disease, we are fit to worship and work for God as he intended. By faith, we can believe that Jesus' blood can wash away every sin, large, medium and small (1 John 1.7), and that his healing power is greater than any sickness or disease (Matt. 4.23) – for would God have created anything greater than himself?

We are not the infirm hoping to get well: we are the healed whom Satan is trying to drag back into the despair of sin and sickness; and the devil stakes everything on the hope that we shall not avail ourselves of Jesus' power and sacrifice.

May we convincingly deprive Satan of that hope.

र्को

The Fourth Sunday of Easter YEAR B

Acts 4.5–12; Ps. 23; 1 John 3.16–24; John 10.11–18

LIFE LAID DOWN

From the gospel: 'For this reason the Father loves me, because I lay down my life in order to take it up again. No one takes it from me, but I lay it down of my own accord. I have power to lay it down, and I have power to take it up again.' (John 10.17–18a)

It may have looked as though Jesus had been deprived of his power when he died on the cross, yet he died 'with a loud voice' (Luke 23.46), in full command of his faculties. His work was not finished: he had business in hell to attend to, and a resurrection to accomplish ... and much else.

We do not know what is going on in the body – or around the body – when a person dies, though we have Jesus' promise that a believer is somehow in Paradise very soon after death (Luke 23.43). That there is less trauma, and a less perceived break in the continuity of living, for the 'departed' is clear: also, we shall know, for ourselves, when our call comes.

And the equanimity that Jesus showed in pursuing God's will, even to death, called forth the Father's love in rich measure. We may argue with God at times – he knows we are not robots – but when his will cuts across ours, then we risk forfeiting his love if we do not redirect our steps into his way. Sometimes it seems a costly step to take, but the alternative could not be borne by our accounts.

र्को

The Fourth Sunday of Easter YEAR C

Acts 9.36–43; Ps. 23; Rev. 7.9–17; John 10.22–30

STILL WATERS

From the psalter: 'The LORD is my shepherd, I shall not want. He makes me lie down in green pastures; he leads me beside still waters; he restores my soul. He leads me in right paths for his name's sake.' (Ps. 23.1–3)

God is love, and even his anger is tempered with mercy. He knows, better than us, how much rest and refreshment we need; and he sees that we reach those still waters exactly when we are ready for them – neither too soon nor too late. Can we not trust him to know best? If your life seems to be shooting the rapids just now, steer as steady a course as you can, for in God's good time you will be brought past the rocks into the still water. We are not to pray for easier lives, but for a right divining of the purpose of God.

We all know people who appear to float perpetually on still water, but there is always at least one factor in anyone's life about which we do not know: they may have great trauma, and yet hide it; or they may be gaining strength and faith for a future challenge. Let God be God in others' lives, and concentrate on navigating your particular stretch of water. Peter was soundly reprimanded when he tried to interfere in another's mission (John 21.22).

❖ The Fifth Sunday of Easter YEAR A

Acts 7.55–60; Ps. 31.1–5, 15–16; 1 Pet. 2.2–10; John 14.1–14

LIVING STONES

From the epistle: 'Come to him, a living stone, though rejected by mortals yet chosen and precious in God's sight, and like living stones, let yourselves be built into a spiritual house, to be a holy priesthood, to offer spiritual sacrifices acceptable to God through Jesus Christ.' (1 Pet. 2.4–5)

When we can see ourselves as living stones in God's house, it is easier to integrate our ministry with that of others. We are not called to be carbon copies of anyone else, still less to covet or envy anyone else's gifts or position. 'Let yourselves be built,' Peter says. Let God mould us and make us what he wants us to be. If we are his, he will do it anyway. It will make the modelling quicker and easier if we co-operate with our Master-builder.

Every single stone in this spiritual house is vital, so that there is no gap, no crumbling, no misfit. How are our corners? Are they smoothly fitted up against our neighbours', or is there friction or a division somewhere? Our subsequent functioning will depend on our compatibility with the place in which God has put us. Do we really believe we are currently where he wants us to be? If not, are we willing for our Builder to relocate us?

The Fifth Sunday of Easter — YEAR B

Acts 8.26–40; Ps. 22.25–31; 1 John 4.7–21; John 15.1–8

CHANCELLOR OF THE EXCHEQUER

From the Acts: 'Now there was an Ethiopian eunuch, a court official of the Candace, queen of the Ethiopians, in charge of her entire treasury. He had come to Jerusalem to worship.' (Acts 8.27)

If, as has been thought, one of the Magi was an Ethiopian, this eunuch may have heard of the special Baby in Bethlehem, some thirty or more years before. Urged by the Spirit, Philip ran to his chariot, and his mission was confirmed by hearing the eunuch reading from the Scriptures.

When we feel God is prompting us to do or say something that may be embarrassing or unusual, do we begin arguing with him, or quickly switch to doing something else, hoping we can forget the still, small voice? In the normal course of things, Philip would probably not get into conversation with a chancellor of the exchequer: but God is a master of the unconventional. How has he surprised you recently?

The eunuch was unlearned in the Scriptures, but that did not discourage him from studying them; nor did his rank prevent him from asking for guidance. We can learn a lot from this chancellor of the Candace's court.

The Fifth Sunday of Easter

Acts 11.1–18; Ps. 148; Rev. 21.1–6; John 13.31–5

A NEW COMMANDMENT

From the gospel: 'Little children, I am with you only a little longer . . .
"Where I am going, you cannot come." I give you a new commandment, that you love one another.' (John 13.33–34a)

Familiarity may dull the impact of this saying. Is loving one another so
alien to our nature as to need a 'new' commandment? And why are
these grown men, with a commission for worldwide evangelism, still
called 'little children'?

True, they had been reborn into Christ's fellowship; and unless they
became as children there was no way they could see the kingdom of
heaven. And is it so surprising to hear these words from Jesus at this
time? Judas has just gone out to do his awful deed. The disciples are
restless. This is Jesus seeking to calm them.

Do we need a new injunction to love one another? There are times
when it is difficult to show love – when people rub us up the wrong way,
or villify us, or misunderstand us, perhaps deliberately. Then we are to
think of a child who has been hurt by another: tears perhaps, a little
temper – and then loving friends again, as if no storm had ever been on
the agenda! Can we do it? Can we afford not to do it?

The command to love is always new – perhaps because we are so
practised in forgetting it.

❖ The Sixth Sunday of Easter

Acts 17.22–31; Ps. 66.8–20; 1 Pet. 3.13–22; John 14.15–21

WHO WILL HARM YOU?

From the epistle: 'Now who will harm you if you are eager to do what is
good? But even if you do suffer for doing what is right, you are blessed
. . . but in your hearts sanctify Christ as Lord. Always be ready to make
your defence to anyone who demands from you an accounting for the
hope that is in you.' (1 Pet. 3.13–14a, 15)

Goodness always seems to rub some people up the wrong way:
motivated by the devil, they lash out at those who are doing right. In

a war situation, no sooner has a breakthrough for peace been initiated than someone throws the peace talks out of kilter, and the whole thing has to start all over again. If we are doing good, we shall run into opposition: nothing is more certain. Are we prepared for the challenge?

We shall need to defend our hope, our faith, many times: and the best preparation for this is to spend as much time as we can in sharing what we believe with our family, priest, congregation and friends. Getting used to talking about our faith is vitally important in these days of bustle and business. In the third and fourth centuries, over much of Asia and the Mediterranean, Christianity had such a high profile that matters of theology and ecclesiastical minutiae were discussed in churches and on the street corners by bishops and butchers alike.

Who would harm us – really harm us – if we talked more about our faith today?

༄

The Sixth Sunday of Easter YEAR B

Acts 10.44–48; Ps. 98; 1 John 5.1–6; John 15.9–17

GOD'S ASTOUNDING GIFT

From the Acts. 'While Peter was still speaking, the Holy Spirit fell upon all who heard the word. The circumcised believers who had come with Peter were astounded that the gift of the Holy Spirit had been poured out even on the Gentiles.' (Acts 10.44–45)

It is a real culture shock when a centuries-old tradition is found suddenly to be obsolete; or perhaps one has made bread in a certain way for years and years, and then one day the well-proven method is thrown awry by an interruption or lapse of memory – yet, surprisingly, the loaves still turn out perfectly; or some seeds are inadvertently sown in the wrong compost – yet germinate and produce an even better crop than when grown in the conventional way. The believers who had dutifully undergone circumcision were astounded when God bypassed the all-important convention and sent his Spirit on to Cornelius and his household! It was to be the start of a worldwide blessing, in which physical circumcision would play no part.

Literally, the Spirit was 'poured out' – given freely and without reserve: not for a time, not to be taken back – but given absolutely, without strings; given in response not only to the faith of Cornelius, but also to the generosity of Peter in sharing his faith with non-Jews.

Are we as generous in the sharing of our faith?

๛

The Sixth Sunday of Easter YEAR C

Acts 16.9–15; Ps. 67; Rev. 21.10, 22—22.5; John 14.23–29 or John 5.1–9

LYDIA OF THYATIRA

From the Acts: 'The Lord opened her heart to listen eagerly to what was said by Paul. When she and her household were baptized, she urged us, saying, "If you have judged me to be faithful to the Lord, come and stay at my home."' (Acts 16.14c–15a)

Luke is there at Philippi, with Paul, and (as in his Gospel) he is interested in a woman coming to faith, Lydia, a seller of the purple cloth for which Thyatira was famous, is used to meeting and dealing with people. Outgoing, with a quick and open mind, she shrewdly assesses the veracity and importance of Paul's preaching, and is not slow to decide publicly for Christ. A woman surely after Paul's heart! One can imagine how he would delight in instructing her to spread the gospel after his mission-team had left Philippi.

Boldness in declaring and sharing our faith – when the time is appropriate and also when it is not (2 Tim 4.2) – is vitally needed today. So we have no Bible group in our street? Well, perhaps someone else will start one. There's a cry, not from Macedonia (Acts 16.9), but from another place in crisis? Well, maybe a church somewhere else will respond. Volunteers are being sought for a children's Fellowship Week of Witness? Hopefully, the next-door parish will find helpers ...

Remember Lydia of Thyatira. She made her own quality decision for God.

❖ Ascension Day YEARS A, B, C

Acts 1.1–11 or Dan. 7.9–14; Ps. 47 or Ps. 93; Eph. 1.15–23; Luke 24.44–53

WIDE AS THE OCEAN

From the Acts: 'So when they had come together, they asked him, "Lord, is this the time when you will restore the kingdom to Israel?" ...

"You will receive power when the Holy Spirit has come upon you; and you will be my witnesses in Jerusalem, in all Judea and Samaria, and to the ends of the earth."' (Acts 1.6, 8)

Still the disciples' minds were locked on to Israel. Jesus tells them gently to prepare for a worldwide mission, for the power of the Spirit is as wide as the ocean, not confined to Judaea, or even Samaria.

We still try to confine God, for there is seemingly an inbuilt desire in the human psyche to explain everything. God refuses to be so limited, particularly on Ascension Day, which is one of the hardest times for preachers! What are we to make of it? Do we accept literally the accounts of Luke? There has yet to be found a 'rational' explanation for the 'lifting up' of Jesus. Perhaps the closest we can get is to liken his ascension to that of a soul at death: we believe it goes to God, but we cannot see its passage or its destination. The difference in Jesus' case was that – at least for part of the journey – he was visible to the disciples.

He has gone, and yet he is here. That is even more of a mystery (Matt. 28.20). It was a transition that – again, mysteriously and miraculously – left the disciples not grieving, but very joyful (Luke 24.52). Alleluia!

❖ **The Seventh Sunday of Easter**   YEAR A
(Sunday After Ascension Day)

Acts 1.6–14; Ps. 68.1–10, 32–35; 1 Pet. 4.12–14; 5.6–11; John 17.1–11

CONSTANTLY PRAYING

From the Acts: 'All these [disciples] were constantly devoting themselves to prayer, together with certain women, including Mary the mother of Jesus, as well as his brothers.' (Acts 1.14)

They had been given a promise by Jesus, and they were not going to let doubt drive them off course again. This was not a re-run of the despair of Good Friday, but of the great joy of seeing Christ ascending to his Father, with the promise of the Holy Spirit. Mary, the other women, the disciples, and even Jesus' brothers who had previously doubted, were maintaining the prayer vigil of their lives.

Prayer strengthens – whether it comes from an individual, family, church or Bible group. Prayer is the bungee-cord linking us to the power of God. Our perception of the link may vary, but the divine elastic of the cord never breaks. Prayer never goes unanswered by God; he always hears; but we need to have faith in his desire to respond, commensurate with our need to ask.

Praying on a one-to-one basis with God probably accounts for most of our prayer-time, but there is a special value and strength in corporate prayer. Perhaps we can increase these times in our services? Or set up more prayer groups in the parish? Today, with the Jerusalem example for our text, is a good time to pray about this.

࿄

The Seventh Sunday of Easter   YEAR B
(Sunday After Ascension Day)

Acts 1.15–17, 21–26; Ps. 1; 1 John 5.9–13; John 17.6–19

GOD'S TESTIMONY

From the epistle: 'Those who believe in the Son of God have the testimony in their hearts. Those who do not believe in God have made him a liar by not believing in the testimony that God has given concerning his Son.' (1 John 5.10)

It is a serious matter not to believe in God: in effect, it is making God a liar, replacing him by Satan who 'is a liar and the father of lies' (John 8.44). Who would turn truth upside down in such a fashion? Well, we can look at the world today and see millions doing just that. Little wonder that in the earliest days of the Church the disciples were accused of 'turning the world upside down'! (Acts 17.6). Truth and falsehood, belief and unbelief, cannot exist together: there is a yawning chasm between them – no fence for the undecided on which to perch!

We who believe have God's convenant (will, testimony) inside us. In order to attack us, Satan has to meet this first – and our Advocate who stands between us and the world *is* that testimony. Jesus *is* the truth of it. 'The one who is in you is greater than the one who is in the world' (1 John 4.4). In this testimony, we have such a power that Satan could (and probably does) accuse us of 'carrying a weapon with intent'! Is it not a privilege to live so dangerously – for God?

࿄

The Seventh Sunday of Easter YEAR C

(Sunday After Ascension Day)

Acts 16.16–34; Ps. 97; Rev. 22.12–14, 16–17, 20–21; John 17.20–26

ONLY BELIEVE

From the Acts: 'Then he brought them outside and said, "Sirs, what must I do to be saved?" They answered, "Believe on the Lord Jesus, and you will be saved, you and your household."' (Acts 16.30–1)

Is it really so simple? Yes – the first step to faith is simply to believe that Jesus is who he is and that he did what he did at Calvary. Do you believe this? Then you are saved. Accept that as a fact, and go on to the next stage, taking to yourself the teaching of Jesus as set out in the Gospels, and learning from the interpretations that the early Church gave to these precepts in the rest of the New Testament. Read, accept, and put into practice.

> If our lives were but more simple,
> We should take him at his word.
>
> (Sir Frederick Faber)

Yet from here the going gets tough, as others wake up to the fact that we are Christians. From now on, we are in a war zone. When we run into opposition, we can take heart that we are doing good, somewhere. To avoid the flak, we can become mediocre. The choice is ours.

But we have been saved. And, in the method of saving us, Jesus was anything but mediocre. In the method of strengthening us and loving us, day by day, he is still anything but mediocre.

❖ Day of Pentecost YEAR A

(Whit Sunday)

Acts 2.1–21 or Num. 11.24–30; Ps. 104.24–34, 35b; 1 Cor. 12.3b–13; John 20.19–23 or John 7.37–39

OTHER TONGUES

From the Acts: 'Divided tongues, as of fire, appeared among them, and a tongue rested on each of them. All of them were filled with the Holy Spirit and began to speak in other languages, as the Spirit gave them ability.' (Acts 2.3–4)

Until now, even with the three major languages of Hebrew, Greek and Latin being understood by many in Judea and its environs, the disciples had been fairly restricted in their mission outlook. Commanded by Jesus to wait in Jerusalem until the Holy Spirit came, they could now go as far as they could travel, the Spirit's gift of languages giving them access to many more potential congregations.

Whenever God calls us to a work, he provides the means to carry it through. Yes, he does – though we may need to take the first step in faith before his help becomes apparent. At our darkest hour, he is still there, showing us where we can dare to look, a way back to normality and growth. Even in our deepest grief, the Spirit is there, telling us simply to believe, to return to the point where our love was strongest, and to rest on God.

He knows our language. He will see to it that eventually we know his.

∾

Day of Pentecost
(Whit Sunday)

YEAR B

Acts 2.1–21 or Ezek. 37.1–14; Ps. 104.24–34, 35b; Rom. 8.22–27; John 15.26–27; 16.4b–15

INTERCESSOR

From the epistle: 'And God, who searches the heart, knows what is the mind of the Spirit, because the Spirit intercedes for the saints according to the will of God.' (Rom. 8.27)

We may look back to the days of monastic Britain, when life for many was less frenetic; but in today's world quick decisions must often be made: instant judgements and reactions. How can we pray ourselves into line with God's Spirit every time? We cannot. We make mistakes and errors of judgement, and inevitably some of these involve other people. But Whit Sunday focuses on the great truth that our indwelling Spirit is present, is here for our benefit, is in direct touch with God, and is stronger than anything that can come against us – and that includes our will.

When we run counter to the Spirit, we must be quick to acknowledge our lapse, and to get back in line with God. He is on our side (Ps.

118.6), he'll meet us halfway. We are not in this battle of wills on our own. But God needs to have his way, and that means a conscious laying-down of our wills, our preferences, and a willingness to be taken over by him, just as the disciples were taken over at Pentecost.

Dare we commit ourselves so far?

৵

Day of Pentecost
YEAR C

(Whit Sunday)

Acts 2.1–21 or Gen. 11.1–9; Ps. 104.24–34, 35b; Rom 8.14–17; John 14.8–17[25–27]

'IF'

From the gospel: 'If in my name you ask me for anything, I will do it. If you love me, you will keep my commandments.' (John 14.14–15)

'If you ask . . . if you love . . .' We have complete freedom of choice, and the wonder is that so many choose to ignore Jesus. The Hebrews called it the *yetzer*, this evil influence that draws us away from God. It is strong, but not as strong as God's Spirit – yet so often the weaker is preferred, because the methods it employs seem to place less initial strain on its followers.

'If . . . if . . .' We can petition God in Jesus' name, and if we love him, we shall ask in line with his laws. Then he will do what he has contracted to do. But if we operate outside his laws, we negate any love we may profess for him, and he is not obliged to accede to our requests.

How do we know we are on course? By applying daily practice to our faith. We grow to understand friends by spending time with them, listening to them, sharing their lives and thoughts. Let us be as attentive to Jesus. Time spent with him is never wasted.

ORDINARY TIME

❖ **Trinity Sunday**   YEAR A

Isa. 40.12–17, 27–31; Ps. 8; 2 Cor. 13.11–13; Matt. 28.16–20

IS IT REALLY SO?

From the gospel: 'When they saw him, they worshipped him; but some
doubted. And Jesus came and said to them, "All authority in heaven
and on earth has been given to me." ' (Matt. 28.17–18)

What do you do when you are leaving your closest, most trusted friends
and colleagues to launch a great enterprise – and some of them are in
two minds as to whether or not to commit themselves? If you are Jesus,
you show them you have real faith that the work will be done.

And the disciples made good. But what a risk God took! And he is
still in the risk business, still choosing the likes of you and me to do the
impossible; still asking us to move mountains. Why? Because Jesus has
dispossessed the devil – so we work on Christian ground. We can fail,
but God cannot fail us. On this Trinity Sunday, when we focus on the
tripartite working of God, let us avail ourselves of all he offers: the more
we ask of him, the more he will ask us to do.

Of course, if we'd rather be also-rans, we can go easy on the prayers.

ะ

Trinity Sunday   YEAR B

Isa. 6.1–8; Ps. 29; Rom. 8.12–17; John 3.1–17

BURNING TOUCH

From the prophets: 'Then one of the seraphs flew to me, holding a live
coal that had been taken from the altar with a pair of tongs. The seraph
touched my mouth with it and said, "Now that this has touched your
lips, your guilt has departed and your sin is blotted out." ' (Isa. 6.6–7)

It can be searingly painful to contemplate turning our lives inside-out
for God. 'Lord, if I have to give up my golf, my television, my
Caribbean holiday ... What if I can't cope with the Bible group, or

the churchwarden's job, or the ministry training course? What if I flunk the hospital visiting, the bereavement counselling? Lord, you can't mean me to give up my home, my job, to go out to... ? Can you?'

The call may not be as insistent or as clear-cut as this. Perhaps just sending a postcard to the Missions may suffice? Remember Isaiah's live coal: it seemed drastic in the extreme – yet he survived. It did not sear him for life, but fitted him for service.

Imagine if he had ducked the challenge!

👁️

Trinity Sunday   YEAR C

Prov. 8.1–4, 22–31; Ps. 8; Rom. 5.1–5; John 16.12–15

SPIRITUAL GUIDE

From the gospel: 'When the Spirit of truth comes, he will guide you into all the truth; ... He will glorify me, because he will take what is mine and declare it to you.' (John 16.13–14)

We may regret not having been with Jesus and able to share his earthly ministry in the same way as the disciples were privileged to do; but Jesus tells us in today's gospel that he did not instruct Peter and the others in everything: he left it to the Spirit to finish the work – and here we can, therefore, share the disciples' experience; like them, we know what it is to go out as Christ's ambassadors – not with our Lord standing physically alongside, but with the all-powerful Spirit in us, teaching and guiding, interceding and sustaining, from the inside out. The disciples were thus equipped to begin worldwide mission. How are we doing, on our smaller pitch?

Jesus did not hand over his teaching seminars to the Spirit because he had run out of time, but because the disciples were not ready for the strong meat of advanced training. God made us, and he knows our abilities and our limitations as no one else does. Can we reflect on how our learning curve at present matches his?

❖ Corpus Christi
YEARS A, B, C

(Thursday After Trinity Sunday)

Gen. 14.18–20; Ps. 116.12–19; 1 Cor. 11.23–24; John 6.51–58

THIS IS MY BODY

From the epistle: 'For I received from the Lord what I also handed on to you, that the Lord Jesus on the night when he was betrayed took a loaf of bread, and when he had given thanks, he broke it and said, "This is my body that is for you. Do this in remembrance of me."' (1 Cor. 11.23–4)

When the Church calls itself 'the body of Christ', it is accepting in full his gift as described here by Paul. Jesus held nothing back, giving his very body for us – physically on the cross, and mystically in the Eucharist. We are called likewise to give everything we have back to God, for his use, in his service. The people whose lives have counted for God may not have been conscious of their sacrifice, but others have benefited from it. When we are on God's business, others are often much more aware of the fact than we ourselves are. Paradoxically, Christ is so close we do not see him, but others see him in us. In the early Church, people observed how Spirit-filled the disciples were, though the disciples did not claim this for themselves.

When we get to that point where we are so abandoned to God that we have lost sight of ourselves, then the 'I and me and my and mine' has been fused into the will of God. Then people will recognize us 'as companions of Jesus' (Acts 4.13).

❖ Proper 4
YEAR A

Gen. 6.9–22; 7.24; 8.14–19; Ps. 46; Rom. 1.16–17; 3.22b–28[29–31]; Matt. 7.21–29

NOT ASHAMED

From the epistle: 'For I am not ashamed of the gospel; it is the power of God for salvation to everyone who has faith.' (Rom. 1.16a)

Can we talk of God to anyone, go anywhere with the gospel, eat as in God's sight, read anything we can share with him? If we can answer 'Yes' to all this, then we, like Paul, are not ashamed of the gospel. We are an open door through which God's power can come and fill us with a surplus for others.

Being proud (in a positive way) of the gospel means that we shall share it in every way that we can; it means that when we hear the gospel being attacked, we are quick to defend it; when God is blasphemed, we bring the word of God to bear on the situation.

There are many parts of the world where the gospel is decried; alien doctrines have taken over, or materialism is rife, or 'natural' disasters have left the terrain as barren as a moonscape, and no creature can survive there any longer. These conditions are an offence against the gospel, and can only be reversed by bringing the gospel back into the situation.

Of ourselves, we can do little to turn the world around to God. But when we team up with the Holy Spirit – when we realize the power that is longing to be put to work from the inside of us – the 'power of salvation' is brought into play.

∂

Proper 4 YEAR B

1 Sam 3.1–10[11–20]; Ps. 139.1–6, 13–18; 2 Cor. 4.5–12; Mark 2.23—3.6

JESUS ONLY

From the epistle: 'For we do not proclaim ourselves; we proclaim Jesus Christ as Lord and ourselves as your slaves for Jesus' sake.' (2 Cor. 4.5)

The psalmist had said: 'Do not let those who hope in you be put to shame because of me' (Ps. 69.6a). There is always a danger of others being attracted to going to a particular church because of someone who is already there, as a worshipper, chorister, organist, preacher, or in any other capacity. We are to encourage new worshippers – yet not to promote our image, but Christ's. If we are standing between anyone and Jesus – whether we have placed ourselves in that position, or others have placed us there – we need seriously to attend to the matter. It is not a question of merely thinking of ourselves as servants of God, but of not thinking of ourselves at all. We are here to present Jesus. He is more than great enough to obliterate our wonderful selves, if we only give him the chance!

Most people want someone whom they can admire, to whose talents and goodness they can aspire. They will elevate other Christians, even themselves. It is our business to show them Christ. He will do the rest.

And, if we are good learners, the business becomes a habit until one day we realize the marvellous ego has been replaced by Jesus.

Or, if we don't realize it, others will!

୶

Proper 4 YEAR C

1 Kings 18.20–21[22–29], 30–39; Ps. 96; Gal. 1.1–12; Luke 7.1–10

SENT BY GOD

From the epistle: 'Paul an apostle – sent neither by human commission nor from human authorities, but through Jesus Christ and God the Father, who raised him from the dead ... Am I now seeking human approval, or God's approval? Or am I trying to please people? If I were still pleasing people, I would not be a servant of Christ.' (Gal. 1.1, 10)

Paul was pressing on, from country to country, coast to coast, meeting local and national authorities, and persecution from all sides; but he had boundless confidence in his calling and commission: it had come from the supreme Authority, and nothing that came against him from anywhere else could annul it or deflect him from his purpose.

Called and chosen by God, only God can decommission us; only he can terminate our contract of employment – and he will, at the very least, consider that possibility if we 'seek human approval', if we 'try to please people'. It is natural to like being liked, but it is not Christian. The glorious paradox is, if we stop trying, and concentrate instead on our work for God, we may well end up with more respect and love; after all, despite current problems, persecution of Christians is usually less drastic today than in Paul's time.

❖ Proper 5 YEAR A

Gen. 12.1–9; Ps. 33.1–12; Rom. 4.13–25; Matt. 9.9–13, 18–26

MERCY, NOT SACRIFICE

From the gospel: 'But when he heard this, he said, "Those who are well have no need of a physician, but those who are sick. Go and learn what this means, 'I desire mercy, not sacrifice.' For I have come to call not the righteous but sinners." ' (Matt. 9.12–13)

'Self-sufficiency' has been a buzz-word for longer than is healthy, and it seems set to stay in fashion. Pride grows, as our dependence on others wanes. But this is contrary to Jesus' gospel. We are not little islands to ourselves: as part of his body, we are meant to integrate, to support, and to be in turn supported. It is not good for our egos, but it is his command. If we are ordinarily human, we need to turn ourselves inside-out and right-way-up for God, or we shall not be recognized as being different from the rest of the world. Christians worth their salt cannot be mistaken for non-believers. We may wear the same clothes, more or less, go to the same places (most of the time), speak the same language (apart from words that do not matter); but even though we are not overtly placarded, the world should know we are different. The difference will make us cry at times. Christians shed more tears than most. But we also have more joy than most, and that means we do more living than most.

৯

Proper 5 YEAR B

1 Sam. 8.4–11[12–15], 16–20 [11.14–15]; Ps. 138; 2 Cor. 4.13—5.1; Mark 3.20–35

DON'T LOSE HEART!

From the epistle: 'So we do not lose heart. Even though our outer nature is wasting away, our inner nature is being renewed day by day. For this slight momentary affliction is preparing us for an eternal weight of glory beyond all measure.' (2 Cor. 4.16–17)

Whatever trauma you are going through now will pass. This may seem cold comfort, if the bills are mounting up, and the food stocks are low. Where is God when we are desperate? Why doesn't he relieve the pressure? Paul gives us the answer: no matter what is coming against us, that which is inside us is being renewed every day. Each morning we start over with God. Can we get through today? Then tomorrow we shall be able to meet the world again.

Often it seems as though God is leaving it too late. Yet somehow we come through the crisis, and looking back we can see he came – perhaps only just in time, but not too late. The Maker of time knows better than anyone how to use it.

Our bodies grow a little older every day, and the time comes when this 'wasting away' is all too obvious. But how is it with our soul? The earlier we begin insuring this for eternity, the stronger it will be when physically we call it a day.

The soul needs far more attention than the body, for it has to last much longer.

෪

Proper 5 YEAR C

1 Kings 17.8–16[17–24]; Ps. 146; Gal. 1.11–24; Luke 7.11–17

BACK FROM THE DEAD

From the gospel: 'Then [Jesus] came forward and touched the bier, and the bearers stood still. And he said, "Young man, I say to you, rise!" ' (Luke 7.14)

It was a very public resurrection, at a high-profile funeral. The 'town called Nain' was left in no doubt as to what had happened, and who was at the centre of it. The young man would die eventually, but meanwhile he was raised to help his mother in her remaining years, and perhaps become a disciple of Jesus himself.

In some parts of the world – particularly Africa and Latin America – the dead are being raised by Christian pastors and healers. People say it is a miracle, and the Church grows. In sophisticated countries like Britain, when the terminally or acutely ill seem to die but then recover, usually medical science is given the credit. Can we blame God if he does not work more miracles?

'Well, it might not work!' And so there is a low priority given to healing and 'raising the dead' in many churches. Are we being consistent in our particular ministry? Or do we blue-pencil the Bible to suit our own preference – or even to bring it up to date?

Gen. 18.1–15 [21.1–7]; Ps. 116.1–2, 12–19; Rom 5.1–8; Matt. 9.35—10.8 [9–23]

ABSOLUTE HEALING

From the gospel: 'Then Jesus summoned his twelve disciples and gave them authority over unclean spirits, to cast them out, and to cure every disease and every sickness.' (Matt. 10.1)

The modern world appears to have difficulty with an uncomplicated verse like this. 'God doesn't do that sort of thing nowadays! Pray to him, by all means, if you have a minor ailment – but leave the mega-germs and epidemics to science!' Even then, with our pills and potions, and tablets and treatment, there is a plethora of hypochondriacs in most societies, for whom nothing is a minor ailment.

Can we believe that God's power is on the wane? Can we credit the notion that some diseases are beyond him? Is it likely that he still has the power to give us eternal life, yet has to admit defeat on the physical front?

Either God has absolute authority, or he has none. If he has none, the devil is in charge, and we haven't a hope in hell.

God allows sickness and disease to afflict us – or to be inflicted on us; and we all die: some twice, most once. Jesus is recorded as having visited Nain just the once; but we can be sure that once was enough for what God wanted done.

> ✌

Proper 6 YEAR B

1 Sam. 15.34—16.13; Ps. 20; 2 Cor. 5.6–10[11–13], 14–17; Mark 4.26–34

HARVEST-TIME

From the gospel: 'He also said, "The kingdom of God is as if someone would scatter seed on the ground, and would sleep and rise night and day, and the seed would sprout and grow, he does not know how ... But when the grain is ripe, at once he goes in with his sickle, because the harvest has come."' (Mark 4.26–27, 29)

God is the Master Gardener. He does not leave any harvest to wither on the plants. When we have done what he has planned for us to do, he will go in with his sickle, and we shall be harvested. There will be times when he seems to call us home, then the illness is healed, the coma is reversed, and life returns for a while. Perhaps this miracle is as much for others' benefit as ours.

We may squander our time and resources, or we may use them well – in which case we shall go to meet our Maker with a fruitful harvest. But let us also remember that what may appear insignificant to us may be vitally important in heaven: the simple kindness, the loving word, a sorrow shared – perhaps long forgotten by us, but remembered by God. We must try our best – but let's not be too hard on ourselves.

God loves us: his sickle has a mercifully soft edge for those who are genuinely his.

ƌ

Proper 6 YEAR C

1 Kings 21.1–10[11–14], 15–21a; Ps. 5.1–8; Gal. 2.15–21; Luke 7.36—8.3

JUSTIFIED THROUGH FAITH

From the epistle: 'We know that a person is justified not by the works of the law but through faith in Jesus Christ ... I have been crucified with Christ; and it is no longer I who live, but it is Christ who lives in me.' (Gal. 2.16a, 19b–20a)

No one was better qualified than Paul to appreciate the strengths and weaknesses of the law. He had sat at the feet of Gamaliel, learning and interpreting scroll after scroll. He had seen the authority that the law could give when he had been harrying the first believers in Christ. And he knew where the law had led him: into a direct confrontation with Jesus. The law was – and is – a dangerous instrument: used as an end in itself, it can negate any value it may possess under wiser usage.

By contrast, faith in Christ gives us insight into the right evaluation and use of the law. We need faith. We can profitably also take on board the law, subsuming it to faith. But we cannot be Christians with the law and no faith.

How is our faith this very day? Are we trusting in anything else?

Gen. 21.8–21; Ps. 86.1–10, 16–17; Rom. 6.1–11; Matt. 10.24–39

SILENCE IS NOT GOLDEN

From the gospel: 'What I say to you in the dark, tell in the light; and what you hear whispered, proclaim from the housetops.' (Matt. 10.27)

Jesus may have cautioned silence after certain healings; but when it came to sharing his teaching, his command was clear: broadcast the good news, loud and clear, on every wavelength possible. At times, this was what the disciples did not want to do for fear of reprisals; but they had to learn that waiting for an opportune time was not what Jesus intended. The gospel must be proclaimed when the time is right, *and* when the time is wrong (2 Tim. 4.2). The gospel transcends time.

We can knock on people's doors, distribute leaflets, stand and preach on a street corner, join a Bible group, church council, synod, train for the ministry, volunteer for mission ... If we make a quality decision to spread the gospel, God will honour it by giving us as many opportunities as we can take; and when we have led even one soul to God, we shall not want to do any lesser work. Let God have his way, and follow where he leads. Be ready to make the most of the circumstances that he engineers. He knows what he is about, and it is his gospel you are dealing with.

෴

Proper 7 YEAR B

1 Sam. 17.[1a, 4–11, 19–23], 32–49; Ps. 9.9–20 or 1 Sam. 17.57—18.5, 10–16; Ps. 133; 2 Cor. 6.1–13; Mark 4.35–41

WITH OPEN HEARTS

From the epistle: 'We have spoken frankly to you Corinthians; our heart is wide open to you. There is no restriction in our affections, but only in yours. In return – I speak as to children – open wide your hearts also.' (2 Cor. 6.11–13)

When, as Christians, we open our hearts to others, we are putting our trust in God. He has brought certain people across our path. He is asking us to be Christ to them. And Christ loved everyone: not even Judas was denied the Last Supper. As children reach out in trust, we are to open our hearts. We have greater experience of the world than a child; so we bring more wisdom to bear on the situation, but we are not to restrict our affections. Paul had suffered much to reach the Corinthians. He was determined to make a success of his mission; to work harder than the other disciples, so that God's grace did not prove to have been bestowed on him in vain.

Are we making the most of God's grace? Are our hearts wide open to the daily challenge, reaching out to those on the margins of society; to the grieving, the sick, the poor and lonely – as well as to those sitting next to us in worship?

ॐ

Proper 7 YEAR C

1 Kings 19.1–4[5–7], 8–15a; Ps. 542–43; Gal. 3.23–29; Luke 8.26–39

ONE IN CHRIST

From the epistle: 'There is no longer Jew or Greek, there is no longer slave or free, there is no longer male and female; for all of you are one in Christ Jesus.' (Gal. 3.28)

Divisions that are of man's making account for much of the world's anguish. Our nationality, station and gender is basically determined for us (though freedom can become slavery, and vice versa); but God does not see divisions within his Church. We are either believers or we are not believers. Any other divisions are irrelevant.

We are slow to learn this lesson. The first-century Christians had problems with favouritism (Jas. 2.1ff.), and it is still rife. The 'ethnic cleansing' of today's dictators is a manifestation of man's inability to ignore differences of creed, culture or circumstances. When will we learn to live as brothers?

If the Church does not give a lead, the situation will not improve. We preach a universal gospel, and consistency dictates that we practise what we preach. Are we caring for the poor in our parish? Do men and women have equal rôles in worship, work, witness and other aspects of parochial life? Are those of other countries welcomed as fellow members of the body of Christ? It may be so in theory, but has the practical implementation caught up with the theoretical?

❖ Proper 8 YEAR A

Gen. 22.1–14; Ps. 13; Rom. 6.12–23; Matt. 10.40–42

A CUP OF WATER

From the gospel: 'Whoever gives even a cup of cold water to one of these little ones in the name of a disciple – truly I tell you, none of these will lose their reward.' (Matt. 10.42)

While we can, let us help all we can. It simply means putting others first, every time. It may only be in the simplest of ways; but if we do what we can, in God's name, out of love for him, he will transform the smallest service into something lastingly beautiful: an entry in his Book of Life, which can never be erased.

The power of positive thinking was, in its day, hailed as a breakthrough in the search for a healthier way of living; and certainly it has helped many who would otherwise have succumbed to the pressures of life. But it is only a part of the real solution: even a non-believer can think positively. We need to involve God in all our thinking, letting his divine alchemy accomplish what we cannot, as he not only transforms situations, but produces them – situations where we can show not our love, but his; not our talents, but his; not our generosity, but his. When we act in his name, out of love for him, we are bringing others into contact with him, and opening the door for him to move powerfully in their lives, as well as in ours.

We are on the road to heaven – not in intention, but actuality.

❧

Proper 8 YEAR B

2 Sam. 1.1, 17–27; Ps. 130; 2 Cor. 8.7–15; Mark 5.21–43

BECOMING RICH

From the epistle: 'For you know the generous act of our Lord Jesus Christ, that though he was rich, yet for your sakes he became poor, so that by his poverty you might become rich.' (2 Cor. 8.9)

We cannot comprehend the glories that Jesus left in order to accept earthly limitations for thirty-odd years – even though prophecies like Isaiah and the apocalyptic writings give us glimpses of the heavenly splendour.

If he, the Lord of glory, was content to live simply so that we may live simply and for ever, how can we justifiably expend our precious God-given energies in running after the temporary riches that this earth has on offer? While God does not require us to live in penury, how can we find justification in his word for an accumulation of wealth or possessions, unless these are used in his service for the benefit of others?

Can we take time today to reflect on how we are using our resources in his service? Jesus gave freely of all he had: time, teaching and talents; and he crowned his giving with his very self – his body and his blood – so that he could gain for us what he already had: eternal life. Can we give less than all we have, for him, to others, in his name? While we keep our heavenly account in credit, he will honour our commitment.

၌

Proper 8 YEAR C

2 Kings 2.1–2, 6–14; Ps. 77.1–2, 11–20; Gal. 5.1, 13–25; Luke 9.51–62

BURYING THE DEAD

From the gospel: ' "Lord, first let me go and bury my father." But Jesus said to him, "Let the dead bury their own dead; but as for you, go and proclaim the kingdom of God." ' (Luke 9.59b–60)

The rabbis used to say: 'Whoever indulges in grief to excess over his dead will weep for another (i.e. himself)' (TB *Moed Katan*, 27b). The man who came to Jesus may simply have wanted to stay at home until his father died, and then to fulfil the duties of burial as the law required; but the call of Jesus cut across legal convention.

The message is simple: we are to put the proclamation of God's kingdom before all else. Do we?

It is so simple, does it take you by surprise?

Jesus is implicitly inviting us to examine our attitude to death. How much of our funeral and bereavement observances are ritual and convention? Do we prolong the grief? Do we focus too much for too long on the eulogy, the obituary, the printed services and acknowledgements? Jesus' words to this man come as a shock, to a society that has become practised in demonstrable bereavement.

Miss me a little, but not too long;
Miss me, but let me go.

Give due thanks for the life of the deceased; mourn for that loss 'of the touch of a vanished hand, and the sound of a voice that is still' – but rejoice that the 'departed' has arrived back in God, and that we still have life and breath to continue working for Christ here and now.

❖ Proper 9 YEAR A

Gen. 24.34–38, 42–49, 58–67; Ps. 45.10–17 or *Canticle:* Song of Sol. 2.8–13; Rom. 7.15–25a; Matt. 11.16–19, 25–30

REACHING OUT

From the gospel: 'But to what will I compare this generation? It is like children sitting in the marketplaces and calling to one another, "We played the flute for you, and you did not dance; we wailed, and you did not mourn."' (Matt. 11.16–17)

The people were so preoccupied they had not noticed whether the children were playing at weddings or funerals. Children crave attention and affirmation (as do we, but we show our eagerness less overtly).

Too busy with living to see the children – or to realize that the Son of God was in their midst! Surely, *we* should not have been so blinkered! Yet what is going on around us today? Can we recall who sat near us at church last Sunday? Who did we pass on the way here this morning? What was reported on the television news last night? There is so much happening in our little part of the universe – and God has placed us in the middle of it, to be his eyes and ears, his hands and feet, his love and his mouthpiece. What a commission! But he has contracted to give us all the time we need to do the work.

The children – *his* children – still dance and call and weep; but 'compassion fatigue' is not part of God's vocabulary.

✂

Proper 9 YEAR B

2 Sam. 5.1–5, 9–10; Ps. 48; 2 Cor. 12.2–10; Mark 6.1–13

PAUL'S THORN

From the epistle: 'Therefore, to keep me from becoming too elated, a thorn was given me in the flesh, a messenger of Satan to torment me, to keep me from being too elated. Three times I appealed to the Lord ... but he said to me, "My grace is sufficient for you, for power is made perfect in weakness." ' (2 Cor. 12.7b–9a)

It does not matter what precisely Paul's thorn consisted of, nor whether it was physical or spiritual. It was frustrating, even humiliating – but it was not life-threatening, nor did it prevent him from continuing with his mission work. God is no sadist: he does not commission us and then make it impossible for us to fulfil our calling.

But we can write our own resignation, by giving way to pride, to an over-high opinion of ourselves. We know Paul was conscious of the fact that he worked harder than the other disciples (1 Cor. 15.10); he travelled far and wide; many would praise his sermons; the ingredients were there for at least a modicum of elation. But God safeguarded his chosen apostle from danger, by allowing the thorn in the flesh.

God is no respecter of persons; he will do the same for us.

But perhaps we are in no danger of becoming elated, or giving way to pride?

❧

Proper 9 YEAR C

2 Kings 5.1–14; Ps. 30; Gal. 6.[1–6], 7–16; Luke 10.1–11, 16–20

SATAN'S FALL

From the gospel: 'The seventy returned with joy, saying, "Lord, in your name even the demons submit to us!" He said to them, "I watched Satan fall from heaven like a flash of lightning." ' (Luke 10.17–18)

While we are quietly doing our Christian duty, bringing souls to God, sharing the gospel, joying with the joyful, weeping with the grief-stricken, helping, comforting, encouraging, in Christ's name, Jesus is watching the mayhem and the confusion in the satanic world. Is there not a positive satisfaction in the thought that our Christian work is giving the devil trouble!

If we could see the devastation, perhaps we should be spurred on to work ever harder for God; but perhaps the sight is too great for human eyes. This is a precious glimpse of the extent to which our work impacts on the spiritual world. Jesus was – and is – giving his disciples great encouragement.

We all need a lift, every so often, to keep going. No one can sustain work year in, year out, given no encouragement. While we soak up every ounce we are given, let us not forget to encourage others whenever we can.

❖ Proper 10

Gen. 25.19–34; Ps. 119.105–112; Rom. 8.1–11; Matt. 13.1–9, 18–23

ALIVE IN GOD

From the epistle: 'If the Spirit of him who raised Jesus from the dead dwells in you, he who raised Christ from the dead will give life to your mortal bodies also through his Spirit that dwells in you.' (Rom. 8.11)

The very calmness with which Paul sets this out is astounding. Jesus has been raised, so we shall have life – not only in the Hereafter, but now: we shall be lit up from the inside, with power to live as God wants us to live, to accomplish what he has planned for us to do before we end our time on earth. This is, of course, providing the Spirit lives in us.

We cannot work for God, or even praise him, unless we have his Spirit. Without the Spirit, the best we can do is to know *about* God. This will not get us very far: even Satan has reached that stage. Many of those with whom we share the gospel will need to divine whether they have 'book-knowledge' or 'Spirit-knowledge' of the Lord.

We can pray for spiritual guidance, in the committed intention to make as much use as possible of our indwelling Spirit. He, and he alone, can help us to realize our spiritual potential. He is willing and able. Are we?

৵

Proper 10

2 Sam. 6.1–5, 12b–19; Ps. 24; Eph. 1.3–14; Mark 6.14–29

MYSTERY MADE KNOWN

From the epistle: 'With all wisdom and insight he has made known to us the mystery of his will, according to his good pleasure that he set forth in Christ.' (Eph. 1.8b–9)

Each day, God takes us a little further into his will. Can we get excited about each day's quota of spiritual knowledge? Can we thrill to think that every morning the mystery of God's will becomes a little better known?

To lose the gift of excitement where our faith is concerned is to be tired of life itself.

At times, certainly, the mystery may seem to deepen. It is then that we have to trust more, not less.

> With mercy and with judgement,
> My web of time he wove,
> And aye the dews of sorrow
> Were lustred by his love;
> I'll bless the hand that guided,
> I'll bless the heart that planned,
> When throned where glory dwelleth,
> In Immanuel's land.
>
> (A. R. Cousins)

In the divine wisdom and insight, our lives are constantly being assessed as God gives us opportunities to suit our potential, and strength to meet our challenges. We can thus have the utmost confidence that each day is tailor-made for our spiritual advancement.

ॐ

Proper 10   YEAR C

Amos 7.7–17; Ps. 82; Col. 1.1–14; Luke 10.25–37

BEARING FRUIT

From the epistle: 'For this reason, since the day we heard it, we have not ceased praying for you and asking that you may be filled with the knowledge of God's will in all spiritual wisdom and understanding, so that you may lead lives worthy of the Lord, fully pleasing to him, as you bear fruit in every good work and as you grow in the knowledge of God.' (Col. 1.9–10)

Paul is nothing if not thorough. Look how he describes the Christian life: *filled* with knowledge ... in *all* ... *fully* pleasing ... in *every* good work ... *grow* in ... knowledge. This is 100 per cent commitment: thrilling stuff, of which saints are made.

God keeps a roll-call of these saints. Your name is on it, and so is mine. By calling and choosing us, God has implied that we have the spiritual potential necessary for qualifying as saints. How are we presently shaping up? Fortunately, we don't have to make the final assessment – for we are often our sternest critics, and the fruit we bear is generally appreciated more by others than ourselves. Our job in life is not to court popularity or approbation, but to be Christ to others: to be a Good Samaritan, when the rest of the world goes by unheeding.

Sitting still and wishing never made a person great;
The good Lord sends the fishing, but we've to dig the bait.

The conditions for sainthood are stringent, but the rewards are eternally glorious.

❖ Proper 11 YEAR A

Gen. 28.10–19a; Ps. 139.1–12, 23–24; Rom. 8.12–25; Matt. 13.24–30, 36–43

GOD'S CHILDREN

From the epistle: 'For all who are led by the Spirit of God are children of God. For you did not receive a spirit of slavery to fall back into fear.' (Rom. 8.14–15a)

Fear is one of the curses of modern society; it has been around since Adam, but today it is stronger than ever before. It creeps into every aspect of life, and causes misery as it establishes and intensifies. There is one way to fight and overcome it: in the power of God's Spirit.

Some try to tell us that a little fear is healthy, but this is unbiblical. Fear is contrary to the will of God, and it is significant that fear (cowardice) heads the list of those who will go to eternity in the lake of fire (Rev. 21.8). We are to have respect for God (a 'holy fear', if you like); but if we accept fear into any other part of our lives, we are implicitly showing respect for Satan.

Are we carrying any fear right now? Fear of illness, poverty, loss, rejection, break-up of relationships, even a fear that we are not loving God as we should? Many fears prove to be groundless; many can be resolved by sharing them with a friend; let us bring the rest to God today, allowing that there is no fear beyond his Spirit's power to heal . . .

Fear is an illness: if we accept it into our bodies, it will do us harm.

❧

Proper 11 YEAR B

2 Sam. 7.1–14a; Ps. 89.20–37; Eph. 2.11–22; Mark 6.30–34, 53–56

BEYOND HOPE

From the epistle: 'Remember that you were at that time without Christ, being aliens from the commonwealth of Israel, and strangers to the covenants of promise, having no hope and without God in the world.' (Eph. 2.12)

What a dreadful state to be in! And, were it not for the coming of Jesus, we should be in that predicament today: faithless, strangers, hopeless and godless. We owe everything to Christ. How often do we tell him so, and thank him?

There are crises in our lives – such as fire, accident or illness – and recovery from such things gives us a great impetus to move mountains for God. Surely, the recollection of what Jesus has done for us should constantly keep us on our spiritual toes! We are, in general, much more ready to ask God for things than simply to say 'Thank You'; but, father-like, how much he must love to be shown gratitude!

If we have a friend who has lost faith, we know how much we grieve, and how hard we work to restore that faith. Can we imagine how God felt, on a worldwide scale, when the hopelessness of the situation prompted him to send Jesus to halt the decline?

Let this immeasurable love give us hope to bring to the hopeless, and the gospel's light to those who are heading into Satan's darkness.

❧

Proper 11 YEAR C

Amos 8.1–12; Ps. 52; Col. 1.15–28; Luke 10.38–42

KITCHEN-SINKERY

From the gospel: 'But the Lord answered her, "Martha, Martha, you are worried and distracted by many things; there is need of only one thing.

Mary has chosen the better part, which will not be taken away from her."' (Luke 10.41–42)

Martha had grown up in a culture where hospitality had a high profile, and where it was unthinkable that a guest would not be offered the best possible meal. But Mary had rightly divined her priorities. The word of Jesus would survive the grave; kitchen-sinkery has much less stamina.

That the rebuke was kindly meant is seen in Jesus' repetition of Martha's name; and she would realize, with hindsight, that the Lord who could feed several thousand with a schoolboy's rations could have produced a meal without Martha doing anything in the kitchen.

Do we put a higher priority on anything other than the word of God? Sometimes work *for* God can choke out time we would otherwise spend in studying his word. Service is important, but today's gospel is a warning against neglecting quiet listening and reflecting on the Scriptures. Jesus did more work for God than anyone else could have accomplished in the time; but he knew when to withdraw for quality time alone with his Father.

❖ **Proper 12**   YEAR A

Gen. 29.15–28; Ps. 105.1–11, 45b or Ps. 128; Rom. 8.26–39; Matt. 13.31–33, 44–52

LEAVENING THE WHOLE

From the gospel: 'He told them another parable: "The kingdom of heaven is like yeast that a woman took and mixed in with three measures of flour until all of it was leavened."' (Matt. 13.33)

God's kingdom is on a grander scale than we can presently imagine. The woman's three measures of flour would make enough bread to feed around a hundred and sixty people: a great quantity for one person to prepare – yet a very small quantity of yeast could leaven the whole dough mass. Similarly, the kingdom of heaven is for a vast number of souls: yet it took only one life, at Calvary, to open its gates to universal entrants.

In a community, the leavening process is often begun by one person. We are all called to take the leaven of the gospel into a world that without it cannot rise to meet God's challenge. A little of the gospel may be all that is needed to begin leavening a great quantity of people. We may start from such a small beginning that, until we have progressed in the leavening, our impact is not apparent. But we need to start: until the yeast has been introduced into the flour, no leavening can begin.

Have we made a start, in faith? Or are we being leavened by someone who has already been activated by God? As the yeast works largely unseen, our leavening cannot always be measured by the ecclesiastical headlines.

∽

Proper 12   YEAR B
2 Sam. 11.1–15; Ps. 14; Eph. 3.14–21; John 6.1–21

KNOWING THE UNKNOWABLE

From the epistle: 'I pray that you may have the power to comprehend, with all the saints, what is the breadth and length and height and depth, and to know the love of Christ that surpasses knowledge, so that you may be filled with all the fulness of God.' (Eph. 3.18–19)

When we are filled to capacity with God's abundance, there is nothing we cannot know of the love of Christ: yet this love is unknowable in the natural realm. By what divine alchemy, therefore, is it possible to know the unknowable? Surely by the power of the Spirit inside us.

Constantly, the Christian is to press in to God's will, to seek more knowledge of Christ, to grow in grace, to spread the gospel. Are we dedicated to all this? If not, what is coming between us and full commitment? It was the love of Christ that bought our freedom, our pardon and our hope: we have a vested interest, surely, in living as completely as we can in this love.

The disciples experienced a miraculous feeding, an awe-inspiring storm-stilling – and much more. Yet still they complained that Jesus' teaching was 'difficult' (John 6.66). It is. Jesus asks us to accept him with the freshness and trust of a child, but he does not patronize us by confining us to the kindergarten for ever.

∽

Hos. 1.2–10; Ps. 85; Col. 2.6–15[16–19]; Luke 11.1–13

PERSISTENCE IN PRAYER

From the gospel: 'I tell you, even though he will not get up and give him anything because he is his friend, at least because of his persistence he will get up and give him whatever he needs.' (Luke 11.8)

Arrow prayers, in an emergency, are probably all we have time for; but in our daily prayer-life, we need to order our case with care and respectful persistence. God is asking here for our whole will to be behind each prayer: we must not be like the lukewarm folk of Laodicea (Rev. 3.16).

And the reward for prayerful persistence? God promises to give us whatever we need. That may be different from what we think we desire, but surely we can trust him not to see us in need. He is preparing us for what he is preparing for us, and he knows what he is about.

If we believe that the thing for which we are asking is indeed in line with God's will, then for however long it takes we are to persist in prayer for it. God does not confine his choice of frontline troops to the actively valiant: there are also many great prayer-warriors there, and always room for more.

Have we some time ago let go of a petition that meant a lot? Perhaps now is the time to revive our perseverance!

❖ Proper 13   YEAR A

Gen. 32.22–31; Ps. 17.1–7, 15; Rom. 9.1–5; Matt. 14.13–21

WRESTLING WITH GOD

From the patriarchs: 'Then he said, "Let me go, for the day is breaking." But Jacob said, "I will not let you go, unless you bless me." … "I have seen God face to face, and yet my life is preserved."' (Gen. 32.26, 30b)

What would our earthly fathers think if we approached them every time crawling on all fours, and addressing them in hushed whispers, begging for a tiny crumb – if such could possibly be spared?

God has given us vitality, the capacity for joy, confidence – yes, respect and love – and spontaneity: qualities that Jacob showed, as he wrestled, both physically and mentally, with the unknown. We come to God as Father, through a Mediator Jacob did not know; but do we come with respectful confidence, as loving, trustful, *natural* children, with spontaneous joy and hope? Do we come for no other reason than that we *love* him? Just *love* God, and tell him so, until his power lifts you off your spiritual feet! Let us get some enthusiasm and daring into our faith! The psalmist begged God 'wondrously' to show his love (Ps. 17.7); dare we make this our prayer today?

❧

Proper 13   YEAR B

2 Sam. 11.26—12.13a; Ps. 51.1–12; Eph. 4.1–16; John 6.24–35

GIFTS FOR MINISTRY

From the epistle: 'The gifts he gave were that some would be apostles, some prophets, some evangelists, some pastors and teachers, to equip the saints for the work of ministry, for building up the body of Christ, until all of us come to the unity of the faith and of the knowledge of the Son of God.' (Eph. 4.11–13a)

'Do not work for the food that perishes,' Jesus ordered (John 6.27), and the author of today's epistle enlarges on why God's gifts are given so liberally, so variously; it is for one purpose: the work of ministry.

Have we lost sight of the point of the divine exercise? Are we wasting some of our gifts on work that is not covered in these verses? It is not too late to redirect our energies. Let's pray for a revival, and let it begin with us.

There is much good being done, in parishes all over the world, but there is still much more to be done. As in the days of the early Church, Christian growth is often best seen in areas where the Church is suffering persecution: overt danger is generally less complicated to fight than covert apathy and indifference. Whichever battlefront we are on, let us try to use all the gifts we have to give a good account of our ministry.

❧

Proper 13 YEAR C

Hos. 11.1–11; Ps. 107.1–9, 43; Col. 3.1–11; Luke 12.13–21

DANGEROUS PROVISION

From the gospel: 'And I will say to my soul, "Soul, you have ample goods laid up for many years; relax, eat, drink, be merry." ' (Luke 12.19)

In the current financial situation, with pension plans, insurances and credit variations growing faster than ever before, this verse has a very modern ring; leisure is big business – but it needs finance, and there are plenty of people telling us how the life of luxury can be lived.

God makes long-term plans too: far longer than earthly insurances can reach; but he will not be restricted to allowing us to see all our long-range schemes through. As James wisely reminds us: 'Instead you ought to say, "If the Lord wishes, we will live and do this or that" ' (Jas. 4.15). We are so insecure that trusting God for a day at a time seems fraught with danger.

Was there not a time when the thought of danger spurred one on to take the challenge?

Leisure is not bad in itself: on occasion, Jesus would take his friends apart for a time of relaxation, and he was not averse to attending festivities and celebrations; but when leisure takes over time that could be spent in God's work, we need to take a long, hard look at our schedule.

❖ Proper 14 YEAR A

Gen. 37.1–4, 12–28; Ps. 105.1–6, 16–22, 45b; Rom. 10.5–15; Matt. 14.22–33

BLOWING IN THE WIND

From the gospel: 'He said, "Come." So Peter got out of the boat, started walking on the water, and came toward Jesus. But when he noticed the strong wind, he became frightened, and beginning to sink, he cried out, "Lord, save me!" ' (Matt. 14.29–30)

Peter did not recognize Jesus at first, but then challenged the Lord to prove his identity by asking the impossible; so, by the time his crisis arrived, Peter could pray, unhesitatingly: 'Lord, help!' Isn't there something of Peter in every Christian today?

No one knew better than a fisherman that you could not walk on water. And yet Peter did it. He did the impossible – until he took his eyes off Jesus and thought about the wind.

Nothing in nature can come between us and God unless we choose to let it come between us. While we live, we can keep focused on God; when we die, through Christ we can have confidence that we shall be wholly his. Can we not gain confidence *now*, in believing this great truth? Can we resolve for one day at a time – or even for one hour at a time – to let nothing come between us, or deflect us, or distract our attention from our Lord? The answer may indeed be blowing in the wind, but is it God's answer or someone else's?

ও

Proper 14 YEAR B

2 Sam. 18.5–9, 15, 31–33; Ps. 130; Eph. 4.25—5.2; John 6.35, 41–51

RIGHTEOUS ANGER?

From the epistle: 'Be angry but do not sin; do not let the sun go down on your anger, and do not make room for the devil.' (Eph. 4.26–27)

It is not a sin to get angry – in a good cause. Jesus showed anger against the devil's work of sickness, disease, craftiness and sin. He took a whip to the entrepreneurs who were violating his Father's house; he could reprimand even his closest friends in no uncertain terms. He had no hesitation in caustically referring to the ecclesiastical hierarchy of his day as 'hypocrites' and 'whitewashed tombs' – and he nicknamed the wily Herod 'that fox'.

That was righteous anger: anger in the cause of God. It was not letting the devil in, but actively, vigorously keeping him at a distance. Jesus did not lose his cool over the hundred and one irritations that daily threaten to trip us up. He was love personified and deified, and – as the *Amplified Bible* renders John 1.14, he was 'full of grace (favour, loving-kindness) and truth'. He was 'not touchy or fretful or resentful' 1 Cor. 13.5. There are few verses better suited to coping with today's stresses than these.

Jesus had his sights set on his reason for living; he was the bread that would outlive anything the devil could use as temptation. Can we not live for eternity, where even righteous anger will be outmoded?

འ

Proper 14 YEAR C

Isa. 1.1, 10–20; Ps. 50.1–8, 22–23; Heb. 11.1–3, 8–16; Luke 12.32–40

THE HEART'S TREASURE

From the gospel: 'Do not be afraid, little flock, for it is your Father's good pleasure to give you the kingdom. Sell your possessions, and give alms.... For where your treasure is, there your heart will be also.' (Luke 12.32–33a, 34)

We are amassing healthy bank accounts and luxuriously appointed houses, yet in a few years we shall have moved on; or are we planning, somehow, to take this earthly treasure with us?

A lady healed of cancer was being interviewed on the television. She was asked how the experience had changed her. 'Before I was ill,' she replied, 'I worried about everything. Now, I'm just so thankful to be alive and well, it doesn't even matter if the roof leaks.'

God in his mercy does not bring each of us through a traumatic illness to get us to that point. Nor does he ask everyone to convert goods and chattels into alms: only his 'little flock' – those who are fully committed to his cause, those who prize the gifts of the Spirit, and who can leave all else behind without regret.

Of course, these may even include you, and me.

❖ Proper 15 YEAR A

Gen. 45.1–15; Ps. 133; Rom. 11.1–2a, 29–32; Matt. 15.[10–20], 21–28

DISTURBER OF THE PEACE?

From the gospel: 'And his disciples came and urged him, saying, "Send her away, for she keeps shouting after us." ... But she came and knelt before him, saying, "Lord, help me." ' (Matt. 15.23b, 25)

She was disrupting the peace of his mission-team, and the annoyed disciples did not mind her hearing their complaint. '*You* tell her, Lord!'

Frustration had severely diluted good manners and respect. What does it take to put us in a similar predicament?

There may be clapping, dancing, speaking in strange tongues . . . and we protest (inwardly, maybe): 'Tell them, Lord, we don't *do* this in a normal service!' Can we not let God be God in others, as well as in ourselves?

The Canaanite woman was persistent, quick of repartee – and faithful. She would go to any lengths to get what she wanted from the Man she believed could give it. Have we, too, got what it takes? Do we stay in there with Jesus, arguing, pleading – even shouting – our case? 'Come now, let us argue it out,' invites the Lord (Isa. 1.18).

He is meeting us more than halfway.

෨

Proper 15 YEAR B

1 Kings 2.10–12; 3.3–14; Ps. 111; Eph. 5.15–20; John 6.51–58

MELODY-MAKERS

From the epistle: 'Be filled with the Spirit, as you sing psalms and hymns and spiritual songs among yourselves, singing and making melody to the Lord in your hearts.' (Eph. 5.18c–19)

There is so much to be joyful for – and joy is a fruit of the Spirit, given without cost. Even physically speaking, it is better to be joyful than sad, for joy does the body good: and, since a smile uses less muscles than a frown, we are even conserving energy.

Generally, people respond to joy. If we want others to be attracted to Jesus, we need to have joy to offer them. At times, the Church has been criticized for its lack of joy. With millions of people still ignorant of the gospel, we cannot afford to indulge in even pious gloom and grief. Surely our faith uplifts us. Why do we have to act as though it did not?

Having 'the light of heaven' in our face is not reserved for our wake, or the lying-in at the chapel of rest. We need to share the warmth of joy while we have breath to tell everyone the reason: to make melody for God, with God, in God, through God. Or heaven may overtake us as the greatest culture-shock of all time.

෨

Proper 15

Isa. 5.1–7; Ps. 80.1–2, 8–19; Heb. 11.29—12.2; Luke 12.49–56

FOR JOY

From the epistle: 'Let us run with perseverance the race that is set before us, looking to Jesus the pioneer and perfecter of our faith, who for the sake of the joy that was set before him endured the cross.' (Heb. 12.1b–2a)

We look to Jesus all the way, from the beginning to the completing of our faith. He does not desert us at any point on the journey; and through his Spirit we can take on some of the deep joy that saw him through Calvary to the victory beyond the grave. Is it not a boost to our spiritual morale that the odds are stacked so mightily on our winning the race?

Perseverance and endurance undergird all Christian life and witness. The world will not go out of its way to help us: whether overtly or covertly, it will come against us. Our motives will be misunderstood, our integrity impugned, and even our sanity questioned. Jesus 'disregarded the shame'. We have a glorious precedent to follow.

He has warned us to beware when everyone speaks well of us (Luke 6.26). This is possible, even in the super-critical world of today. But if no one is antagonizing, or finding fault with us, we may justifiably question whether we are doing as much for Christ as we could.

❖ Proper 16

Exod. 1.8—2.10; Ps. 124; Rom. 12.1–8; Matt. 16.13–20

GIFTS ACCORDING TO GRACE

From the epistle: 'We have gifts that differ according to the grace given to us: prophecy, in proportion to faith; ministry, in ministering; the teacher, in teaching; the exhorter, in exhortation; the giver, in generosity; the leader, in diligence; the compassionate, in cheerfulness.' (Rom. 12.6–8)

God, the giver who out-gives everyone, initially gives us grace sufficient to learn to use the talent he has chosen for us; then, as our capacity increases, he gives us more grace (Jas. 4.6), until all grace and every blessing is on offer to us (2 Cor. 9.8). This is generosity on the grand scale, but God is determined to get his work done – and we are the only ones in line to do it.

None of the gifts is for our personal use: no one can prophesy or minister to himself – or teach, exhort, or give to himself; or lead or be compassionate to himself. God gives to us, for others – some of whom, in turn, will have been given gifts to share with us.

When we have become so immersed in sharing God's gifts that we do not recognize ourselves, we shall have passed the point of worrying about our image. Others may recognize us as having God's grace. We can leave the rest with God.

ॐ

Proper 16 YEAR B

1 Kings 8.[1, 6, 10–11], 22–30, 41–43; Ps. 84; Eph. 6.10–20; John 6.56–69

GOD'S ARMOUR

From the epistle: 'Stand therefore, and fasten the belt of truth around your waist, and put on the breastplate of righteousness. . . . shoes . . . to proclaim the gospel of peace. . . . the shield of faith . . . the helmet of salvation, and the sword of the Spirit, which is the word of God.' (Eph. 6.14–17)

Truth, righteousness, peace, faith, salvation and the word. We need nothing else, save the will to use this armour that we have been given. God will take care of everything that comes behind us (Isa. 52.12; 58.8). Our job is to press forward.

It is not easy to wear God's armour. Day after day circumstances threaten our peace and joy, and challenge our fight for the truth.

Today's society – though critical in the extreme when attempting to destroy others' reputations and promote gossip – is tolerant of immoralities that even a generation ago would not have been accepted.

In the gospel reading we hear of many disciples absconding from Jesus' mission-team. They could not understand or accept his teaching on his flesh and blood given as life for men. Today, many are still deserting the holy ranks. Do we care about them, enough to try to win them back?

ॐ

Proper 16

Jer. 1.4–10; Ps. 71.1–6; Heb. 12.18–29; Luke 13.10–17

A FIERY GOD

From the epistle: 'Therefore, since we are receiving a kingdom that cannot be shaken, let us give thanks, by which we offer to God an acceptable worship with reverence and awe; for indeed our God is a consuming fire.' (Heb. 12.28–29)

We may call God 'Abba' ('Daddy'), and come to him in confidence, with assurance of faith – for he is love. But we must learn where to draw the line between boldness and familiarity. Because he is God, we also owe him reverence (respect) and awe.

This should not overawe us: rather, it should add to our delight and privilege to do his will. Why, after all, should the Creator of the universe (and, for all we know, countless other universes) even care about us, or want to be loved by us?

Because it cost him so much to save us.

We can never repay the debt of Calvary, but we can do our best. Anything less is to drive another nail into the body of Jesus. That body no longer hangs on a cross. It is called the Church: militant here on earth (and suffering), and triumphant in heaven. And we are a part of this body. Only a moron would knock a nail into himself.

❖ Proper 17

Exod. 3.1–15; Ps. 105.1–6, 23–26, 45c; Rom. 12.9–21; Matt. 16.21–28

MISPLACED SYMPATHY

From the gospel: 'But [Jesus] turned and said to Peter, "Get behind me, Satan! You are a stumbling block to me; for you are setting your mind not on divine things but on human things."' (Matt. 16.23)

Sometimes we have misplaced notions of sympathy. 'Lord, she is such a wonderful Christian! She shouldn't have to suffer as she does!' Or, 'Lord, he really deserved to get that job, why did it go to so-and-so instead of him?' Or, 'Lord, why did she have to die, just before she was released from captivity at the hands of terrorists?' *Why,* Lord?

We are not in Never Never Land, nor where life always goes on happily ever after. But neither are we mere pawns in a chess game played by a sardonic, cynical Grand Master. God's purposes are being worked out, *for* us, in love. We only see the microscropic view; God's is the macroscopic perspective – the view at the end of all the tangles of life's mistakes and trials. If we were the planners, where should we get ourselves, in our efforts to ride round the disasters, the misfortunes and the errors of judgement?

Almost certainly we should drive ourselves so much off course that we'd end up anywhere but within sight of the pearly gates.

გ

Proper 17 YEAR B

Song of Sol. 2.8–13; Ps. 45.1–2, 6–9; Jas. 1.17–27; Mark 7.1–8, 14–15, 21–23

BE UP AND DOING

From the epistle: 'But be doers of the word, and not merely hearers who deceive themselves.' (Jas. 1.22)

Jesus had a perfect right to stay sequestered in the temple, and lecture to anyone who would listen, day after day. Instead, his relatively short three-year ministry was spent in going about doing good. His disciples have generally tried to follow his example for 2,000 years. When monasticism flourished, so too did the criticism that the monk was interested only in the saving of his own soul. However unfounded such criticism may have been – for the monks often opened their houses to the sick and needy – the cloistered life was contrasted with the active, outgoing ministry of Jesus and the disciples of the early apostolic Church.

It is possible to put service for Jesus above worship, though probably this is not dangerously common in modern times. Certainly, most of us could do more for him; equally certainly, more of us than ever before are trying.

Hearing the word, in order to go out and put it into practice, is fine; hearing it when we should be out there actively practising it is procrastination.

Let us reflect, this week, if we have got the balance right.

გ

Proper 17

Jer. 2.4–13; Ps. 81.1, 10–16; Heb. 13.1–8, 15–16; Luke 14.1, 7–14

THE LORD MY HELPER

From the epistle: 'Keep your lives free from the love of money, and be content with what you have; for he has said, "I will never leave you or forsake you." So we can say with confidence, "The Lord is my helper; I will not be afraid. What can anyone do to me?"' (Heb. 13.5–6)

If we have a lot of money, it is for the service of God. If we have a little, it is still for his service. He will not see us destitute: that is a sacred promise, so we should not worry about money. If we worry, it means that money owns us: we are either its slave or its lover. To break either of these bonds, we need to concentrate on our heavenly bank account, which operates a longer-term interest than the TSB or Nat West or Lloyds could ever contemplate.

The following quotation is from Psalm 118.6: 'With the LORD on my side I do not fear. What can mortals do to me?' So how do we *not* worry about money? See again Jesus' attitude to it: the ministry-team had a purse, but Judas, the treasurer, stole from it. Did Jesus castigate him? When Peter had no tribute-money, Jesus sent him to find it – in the mouth of a fish! Will it take us a lifetime to learn how to treat money in the Jesus way?

❖ **Proper 18**   YEAR A

Exod. 12.1–14; Ps. 149; Rom. 13.8–14; Matt. 18.15–20

TWO OR THREE

From the gospel: 'Again, truly I tell you, if two of you agree on earth about anything you ask, it will be done for you by my Father in heaven. For where two or three are gathered in my name, I am there among them.' (Matt. 18.19–20)

If we have faith like a mustard seed, we can move a mountain. Team up with a prayer-partner, and the two of you can surely move a continent! That is why corporate prayer and worship are so important. Jesus showed by example (Luke 4.16) that we neglect this at our peril.

Two people praising or praying in Jesus' name bring him in to make a trio.

> Almighty God, who hast given us grace at this time with one accord to make our common supplications unto Thee; and dost promise, that when two or three are gathered together in Thy name, Thou wilt grant their requests; Fulfil now, O Lord, the desires and petitions of Thy servants, as may be most expedient for them; granting us in this world knowledge of Thy truth, and in the world to come life everlasting. Amen
>
> (St John Chrysostom)

❧

Proper 18   YEAR B

Prov. 22.1–2, 8–9, 22–23; Ps. 125; Jas. 2.1–10[11–13], 14–17; Mark 7.24–37

PRACTICAL FAITH

From the epistle: 'If a brother or sister is naked and lacks daily food, and one of you says to them, "Go in peace; keep warm and eat your fill," and yet you do not supply their bodily needs, what is the good of that? So faith by itself, if it has no works, is dead.' (Jas. 2.15–17)

Faith only lives when translated into practical application. St Teresa of Avila was a devout mystic – yet she could not only set starry-eyed postulants to scrubbing floors, but also rolled up her own sleeves and joined them in the work. 'All for Jesus' is a prayer that transforms even a kitchen floor into something beautiful for God.

Our faith is the means by which we can help others: believers and non-believers. What we do, or do not do, may for them literally be a matter of life and death.

A young aspiring artist sent one of his drawings to the principal of a prestigious art college; it showed a church he had known since childhood. But the sketch, and his application, were turned down. Apparently this rejection preyed on his mind, and the boy who may have risen to be a great artist became instead a megalomaniac hell-bent on destruction.

His name was Adolf Hitler.

May we use our talents not to spurn others, but to help and encourage them.

❧

Proper 18 YEAR C

Jer. 18.1–11; Ps. 139.1–6, 13–18; Philemon 1–21; Luke 14.25–33

THE IMPOSSIBLE IDEAL?

From the gospel: 'So therefore, none of you can become my disciple if you do not give up all your possessions.' (Luke 14.33)

Every one? Jesus does not deal in exceptions here. All means all, and through the centuries since Jesus issued this strict condition many have risen to the challenge – from St Thecla to Mother Teresa, and from St Francis of Assisi to C. T. Studd, the Cambridge cricketer and pioneer.

It is so thoroughgoing, can we bear it? Does 'give up' really mean that? Or can we fulfil our mission by not *relying* on our possessions, yet still using them in God's service? Each of us must seek God's guidance here, trusting him to make clear to us if anything is standing in the way of full commitment. Nothing is more important than loving God; and if we love him passionately, steadfastly and wholeheartedly, we shall find that other things gradually melt into his perspective, not ours. If we love him enough, we shall indeed love nothing else as much. If we love him enough, he will have his way with us, using us in ways so varied and exciting that we shall not miss what we have left behind.

❖ Proper 19 YEAR A

Exod. 14.19–31; Ps. 114 or *Canticle*: Exod. 15.1b–11, 20–21; Rom. 14.1–12; Matt. 18.21–35

CHARITY IN THE CHURCH

From the gospel: 'Then Peter came and said to him, "Lord, if another member of the church sins against me, how often should I forgive? As many as seven times?" Jesus said to him, "Not seven times, but, I tell you, seventy-seven times." ' (Matt. 18.21–22)

The rub here is 'another member of the church'. We may expect angst from non-believers, but surely our fellow-worshippers should be as perfect as we ourselves are! History from every period is telling us that strife beginning from within Christian ranks has, time and again, ended in unholy wars, splitting countries and even continents. Faith brings out

ORDINARY TIME · 105

the best in people, but it also stirs the deepest emotions, which can act as dangerous flashpoints.

Jesus tells us: stop the strife where it starts. Don't let it grow and spread with the speed of light. Forgive the first wrong. Forgive. Forgive. Love, which 'does not insist on its own rights, or its own way' (*Amplified Bible*, 1 Cor. 13.5), must make the first, quick move to forgive – whether it is the wrongdoer or the wronged. If you are right, and in strife, you are wrong! Let go the strife, and forgive – and keep on forgiving.

ॐ

Proper 19 YEAR B

Prov. 1.20–33; Ps. 19 or *Canticle*: Wisd. 7.26—8.1; Jas. 3.1–12; Mark 8.27–38

PERFECT SPEECH

From the epistle: 'For all of us make many mistakes. Anyone who makes no mistakes in speaking is perfect, able to keep the whole body in check with a bridle.' (Jas. 3.2)

At times we could all benefit from an attack of spiritual laryngitis, for we let our tongue carry us into all sorts of trouble, often wounding (however unintentionally) those whom we love the best. While we live, we shall continue to do this, for no one is perfect (Rom. 3.23; 5.12); but God will honour our commitment to try to watch our speech.

It helps if we make an effort to see the best in people and situations: to replace a critical attitude with one of love and tolerance; not to bear a grudge, or to imagine a slight where probably none was intended. There will be times when we are proved wrong – but if we let the insult drop, it will not harm us.

The world has always loved gossip, and today it's a flourishing industry. Can we ignore it? This is the only way to kill an enemy that ruins millions of lives every year. If you cannot walk away from gossip, close your ears and lips to it, and remember: we all make mistakes.

ॐ

Proper 19 YEAR C

Jer. 4.11–12, 22–28; Ps. 14; 1 Tim. 1.12–17; Luke 15.1–10

EACH ONE MATTERS

From the gospel: ' "Rejoice with me, for I have found my sheep that was lost." Just so, I tell you, there will be more joy in heaven over one sinner who repents than over ninety-nine righteous people who need no repentance.' (Luke 15.6b–7)

Just as a sheep was important to the shepherd, and a coin from her bridal chain was precious to the woman, so each repentant sinner means an incalculable amount to God. Can we take this in, that God and the heavenly host get thrilled about us? That we matter to them? That God goes to work on us with a thoroughness that tells of a love beyond comprehension?

The sheep made no effort to get back to the fold, and the coin lay passively waiting for someone to find it. Even before we show any awareness of our plight, God moves to help us: our predicament stirs him to action. This in itself should shame us into repentance.

And we are not perfect: we need to come to God daily, to repent before our little faults grow large. If we are careful of our failings, we shall be more tolerant of others'.

If God can show such spiritual energy concerning us, does it not spur us on to shake off any laziness on our part?

❖ Proper 20 YEAR A

Exod. 16.2–15; Ps. 105.1–6, 37–45; Phil. 1.21–30; Matt. 20.1–16

THIS BELONGS TO ME!

From the gospel: 'Take what belongs to you and go; I choose to give to this last the same as I give to you. Am I not allowed to do what I choose with what belongs to me? Or are you envious because I am generous? So the last will be first, and the first will be last.' (Matt. 20.14–16)

Because God is God, he can bring to birth and cause to die at any time. Because he is God, he continues to give us every chance to do good. Are we to complain because he is choosing what to do with his own?

ORDINARY TIME · 107

Like Peter (John 21.21), we look at others and compare their lot with our own. It is no business of ours, but implicitly we measure our work, advantages and abilities against others'. God will not be limited: he can deal with everyone he has made in a different way – and still have innumerable options left over; or he can deal in the same way with varying lives and abilities – just as he did in today's parable.

The dealing belongs to God. He knows what he is preparing individuals for; and what may seem arbitrary, or even downright unfair, to us is precisely in line with his purpose.

Let's allow that he knows better than we can imagine.

ॐ

Proper 20 YEAR B

Prov. 31.10–31; Ps. 1; Jas. 3.13—4.3, 7–8a; Mark 9.30–37

MORE PRECIOUS THAN JEWELS

From Proverbs: [Concerning a capable wife] 'Strength and dignity are her clothing, and she laughs at the time to come. She opens her mouth with wisdom, and the teaching of kindness is on her tongue.' (Prov. 31.25–26)

Very few of us can laugh at the time to come, or even view it with equanimity. Worry and apprehension characterize much of today's world. So the onus is even more on Christians to make the difference. This ideal woman may be impossible to replicate in every detail; but unless we aim for the highest, we shall not come within miles of it.

The power of the tongue, for good and ill, is emphasized in many scriptures, notably the letter of James. In an age where many feel compelled to say something on every occasion, and where slander is so common that much of it never makes it to the overcrowded court schedules, Christians need as never before to make a stand not only for purity, but kindliness of speech. Our tongues are a good indication of whether it is fair or stormy in our hearts. Let us become well versed in giving fair-weather forecasts, turning the tide of argument, quashing tittle-tattle, and seasoning every word with the salt of the gospel.

ॐ

Proper 20

Jer. 8.18—9.1; Ps. 79.1–9; 1 Tim. 2.1–7; Luke 16.1–13

FOR THOSE IN AUTHORITY

From the epistle: 'I urge that supplications, prayers, intercessions, and thanksgivings be made for everyone, for kings and all who are in high positions, so that we may lead a quiet and peaceable life in all godliness and dignity.' (1 Tim. 2.1–2)

The decisions made by those in authority can affect millions of lives; some have been born to high office, others have had it thrust upon them, and a few have moved mountains to obtain it for themselves. All, however, need our prayers, for much is asked from those to whom much has been given.

We can see today countries governed by those who command respect but no love, and a few who by their conduct have forfeited respect as well as love. Let us hold these rulers before God in prayer, together with those responsible for advising them, and for the people of their countries.

And let us also hold our own monarchy and government – national and local – up in prayer. We have a duty to the secular world of officialdom; for if the good qualities that it possesses can be channelled into Christian service, heaven will be enriched, and – in the short term – so will our world.

❖ Proper 21

Exod. 17.1–7; Ps. 78.1–4, 12–16; Phil. 2.1–13; Matt. 21.23–32

WORK IT OUT

From the epistle: 'Work out your own salvation with fear and trembling; for it is God who is at work in you, enabling you both to will and to work for his good pleasure.' (Phil. 2.12b–13)

Working out what God has worked in takes a lifetime, for he is constantly giving us more to share with others – more to discover about our purpose in life: more knowledge of himself; more grace, more strength, more opportunities for service. He is pruning, training, feeding us, as the 'vine-dresser' encourages his choicest vines to go from strength to strength. We do not realize our spiritual potential this side of the grave, so let's stop persuading ourselves that we have got there.

Paul tells us that before we can do anything for God, we have to be willing to do it. How obvious this seems, yet how often we take up work from a sense of duty, slogging away at it with stoical solemnity. God is not asking for conveyor-belt Christians, but for those on fire with love and eagerness and real joy in their mission. How can we lead others to Christ, if we give the impression that our working out of salvation is merely a test of endurance?

❧

Proper 21 YEAR B

Esth. 7.1–6, 9–10; 9.20–22; Ps. 124; Jas. 5.13–20; Mark 9.38–50

FESTIVAL TIME

From the Old Testament: '[Keep 14–15 Adar] as the days on which the Jews gained relief from their enemies, and as the month that had been turned for them from sorrow into gladness and from mourning into a holiday; that they should make them days of feasting and gladness, days for sending gifts of food to one another and presents to the poor.' (Esth. 9.22)

So was initiated the Feast of Purim, celebrating the foiling of Haman's anti-Semitic plot, and the restoration of Jewish honour under Ahasuerus. The book of Esther is read in synagogue at Purim, in the morning and evening of 14 Adar, and the congregation makes as much noise as it can at each mention of Haman's name. Feasting, the giving of presents, and great rejoicing and donating of charity, characterize the celebration.

Do we make the most of the Christian festivals that punctuate our year? God has given us a great capacity for enjoyment as well as for work, because he knows we need to exercise both gifts in order to function properly. If we cannot joy in God's service, we are not likely to find fulfilment, or to attract others to what we profess is the best calling of all.

❧

Proper 21 YEAR C

Jer. 32.1–3a, 6–15; Ps. 91.1–6, 14–16; 1 Tim. 6.6–19; Luke 16.19–31

THEY WILL NOT BELIEVE

From the gospel: '[Jesus] said to him, "If they do not listen to Moses and the prophets, neither will they be convinced even if someone rises from the dead."' (Luke 16.31)

Jesus was so right; and he is still right. Millions are continuing to careen towards eternity either ignorant of Jesus, or in disbelief that his resurrection has given them the chance of choosing life rather than death. What can you and I, as individuals, do to stop this helter-skelter dash to hell?

Not a lot. But we are not simply individuals. Each of us has the Holy Spirit, with all the power he can give. Together, we are more than able to halt the decline, for God empowers us not merely to cope with the opposition, but to beat it handsomely. If we cannot believe this, there is little point in our sharing the gospel, for we would be asking others to believe what we could not.

The disciples were as slow to comprehend as we sometimes are. In this parable, Jesus was preparing them for his own resurrection. He was also giving them a precious glimpse into the dichotomy of the eternal worlds: where we go when we die is determined by how we have lived; and the grave marks the point of no return.

❖ Proper 22 YEAR A

Exod. 20.1–4, 7–9, 12–20; Ps. 19; Phil. 3.4b–14; Matt. 21.33–46

GIVEN TO OTHERS

From the gospel: '"Now when the owner of the vineyard comes, what will he do to those tenants?" They said to him, "He will put those wretches to a miserable death, and lease the vineyard to other tenants who will give him the produce at the harvest time."' (Matt. 21.40–41)

We are often quick to give advice, especially if someone else stands to be the recipient of our strictures; and at times we even try to tell God what he should be doing in others' lives. Let us mind our own business, for that is usually complicated enough to demand serious attention.

ORDINARY TIME · 111

God is munificent in his giving, but Jesus' parable is a warning that if we mishandle our gifts they can be given to others – not necessarily because they have shown themselves to be more deserving, but because God in his mercy and judgement wants to give them the chance that we have passed up.

What do we do if this has already happened in our lives? Can we find the generosity of spirit to wish these others well? Can we resolve in future to use every single gift God may give us, as fully and as generously as possible? If we can open our hearts this far, God will free us from the past, and fit us for what is to come.

ॐ

Proper 22   YEAR B
Job 1.1; 2.1–10; Ps. 26; Heb. 1.1–4; 2.5–12; Mark 10.2–16

SUSTAINER OF ALL

From the epistle: '[Jesus] is the reflection of God's glory and the exact imprint of God's very being, and he sustains all things by his powerful word.' (Heb. 1.3a)

Consider this world, and all that is in it. Nothing is holding every thing in place, and maintaining life on it, except the all-powerful word of God. And, since that which sustains is greater than what it sustains, Jesus could say with justification that 'heaven and earth will pass away, but my words will not pass away' (Matt. 24.35; Mark 13.31; Luke 21.33). The threefold recording of this emphasizes this saying's importance.

The ether into which God speaks, from creation until the end of the world, is charged with life for this world, the heavens and beyond. Yet this same mighty God says: 'Call me Daddy, for I love you all so much!'

We can obey, joyfully, because Jesus has put a human face on God: we see children flocking to him, men and women accompanying him in his travelling ministry-team; and disciples ecstatic with joy, and full of courage, carrying on his work when he returned to his Father.

This is a God whom we can love.

ॐ

Proper 22

Lam. 1.1–6; *Canticle*: Lam. 3.19–26 or Ps. 137; 2 Tim. 1.1–14; Luke 17.5–10

JOB SATISFACTION

From the epistle: 'For this gospel I was appointed a herald and an apostle and a teacher, and for this reason I suffer as I do. But I am not ashamed, for I know the one in whom I have put my trust, and I am sure that he is able to guard until that day what I have entrusted to him.' (2 Tim. 1.11–12)

Paul had trusted God with his hope and with his life. We cannot trust anyone with more. Job learned to declare: 'Even though he kills me, I will trust him.' Anything less is not trust. God asks for full commitment, or none. The slave in our gospel reading had a hard life, but it was not unbearable. Paul, by our standards, pushed himself beyond normal limits, but he did not die from overwork. Heaven does not wait for couch potatoes, but for those who have been prepared to put God first, with the gifts he has given.

We need never worry about God's image being damaged by work we do for him. He will safeguard his honour – and ours. What matters is not what we have, but what we are; not what happens to us, but how we react to it; not what we can accumulate, but what we can do without for the furtherance of the gospel. God will guard what we have entrusted to him.

❖ Proper 23

Exod. 32.1–14; Ps. 106.1–6, 19–23; Phil. 4.1–9; Matt. 22.1–14

A MOTLEY COLLECTION?

From the gospel: '"Go therefore into the main streets, and invite everyone you find to the wedding banquet." Those slaves went out into the streets and gathered all whom they found, both good and bad; so the wedding hall was filled with guests.' (Matt. 22.9–10)

Isn't this shocking! Perhaps the riff-raff didn't even wash before the banquet! Yet Jesus points to one man who wore the wrong clothes.

Why is it that someone's appearance, rather than his morals, causes eviction from the celebrations?

Surely it is that if morality effected the 'Open Sesame', heaven's road would be thronged with Holy Joes; if physical cleanliness was a prerequisite, the way would be fragrant with perfumers; if fitness was the criterion, first-class athletes would block the pearly gates. As it is, we have to strive not to meet one, two or even three criteria, but simply to be as faithful, in all aspects of our life, as we can – for it may be the most unexpected mistake or lapse that decides our fate. 'Be faithful until death, and I will give you the crown of life,' God tells us (Rev. 2.10).

❧

Proper 23 YEAR B

Job 23.1–9, 16–17; Ps. 22.1–15; Heb. 4.12–16; Mark 10.17–31

THE THRONE OF GRACE

From the epistle: 'For we do not have a high priest who is unable to sympathize with our weaknesses, but we have one who in every respect has been tested as we are, yet without sin.' (Heb. 4.15)

Because Jesus knows how we feel – every time – we can confidently approach his throne, and he will help us when we need assistance: not in advance, as some sort of downpayment, but at the time when help is needed.

Jesus knew how the rich man felt about his possessions, yet that man had only a fraction of the wealth our Lord had known in glory. It had been possible for Jesus to leave heaven's wealth, and he was asking far less from the earthly millionaire. Yet the price was still too high for the rich man.

The disciples were worried about their own sacrifices. Jesus too knew what it was to leave home and family. He was asking less of his friends. For Peter and the others, the price was *not* too high.

How much have we 'paid' to become committed Christians? If we cannot calculate it, let's leave well alone; Jesus knows, and we can trust him to get the balance right. It is one equation we do not need to worry about.

❧

Proper 23

Jer. 29.1, 4–7; Ps. 66.1–12; 2 Tim. 2.8–15; Luke 17.11–19

GRATITUDE

From the gospel: 'Then one of them, when he saw that he was healed, turned back, praising God with a loud voice. He prostrated himself at Jesus' feet and thanked him. And he was a Samaritan.' (Luke 17.15–16)

Gratitude is often an unsung – and too often an unheard – gift, but it has great power. It can turn around a negative situation, heal wounded feelings, and generally smooth life's way. Let us never be mean or forgetful in our use of this precious gift.

The fact that the only leper to show gratitude was one of the hated Samaritans would fix the incident even more firmly in the minds of Jesus' disciples. Perhaps the other nine were grateful, but they did not have the courtesy to express their thanks. So often we ask God for things, but forget to thank him when we receive them. In the 'ACTS' of prayer, gratitude comes before any further requests:

Adoration
Confession
Thanksgiving
Supplication

If our prayers are to be meaningful, let's get our 'ACTS' together.

❖ # Proper 24

Exod. 33.12–23; Ps. 99; 1 Thess. 1.1–10; Matt. 22.15–22

KNOWN ABROAD

From the epistle: 'For the word of the Lord has sounded forth from you not only in Macedonia and Achaia, but in every place your faith in God has become known.' (1 Thess. 1.8a)

Wherever the Roman currency was used, the head of Caesar was seen on every coin. In his letter to the Christians at Thessalonica, Paul is talking of a better communications network: the work of faith. This was spreading out from these new Christians at a rate of knots, and Paul is vibrantly generous in his praise and encouragement.

For even a little encouragement goes a long way. We can expend so much energy in God's service that we become weary, and even disheartened. Then a cheering word, a sincere thank-you, a helpful, appreciative hand, a shared testimony, and we are recharged, rethrilled, to meet the next task with fresh energy.

Work for God is never wasted, even though in the short term it may go unnoticed, misunderstood, or taken for granted. Someone notices and understands, and even the smallest work we do may affect many lives – or even one – for good.

Reflect today on the encouragement Paul's letter would give to the Thessalonians: how they would treasure it, reading it week by week in their services.

≈

Proper 24   YEAR B

Job 38.1–7[34–41]; Ps. 104.1–9, 24, 35c; Heb. 5.1–10; Mark. 10.35–45

A PRIEST FOR EVER

From the epistle: ' "You are my Son, today I have begotten you"; ... "You are a priest forever, according to the order of Melchizedek." ' (Heb. 5.5b, 6b)

Were you there 'when the morning stars sang together and all the heavenly beings shouted for joy?' (Job 38.7). Were you there when the priestly order, typified by Melchizedek, was founded? No – but the work begun then still continues, and you are very definitely a part of it now.

Melchizedek comes out of the mists of history to visit Abraham and accept his tithes; then, a few verses later, he slips back into history. But he leaves a royal priesthood, and a legacy that will encompass the universe. He is of a world where stars dance and sing, and where angel voices are strong enough to shake the doors of heaven (Isa. 6.4): an exciting world, with such movement, joy and light as we have never experienced. It is a world that defies imagination: God's world, from where Jesus came to limit himself for 30 years in order to give us the hope that one day we would inherit heavenly citizenship. Once perfected by his sacrifice, Jesus opened the door to our perfecting, which means we are 'a kingdom, priests serving God' (Rev. 1.6; 5.10). It is God's seal on our ministry.

≈

Proper 24 YEAR C

Jer. 31.27–34; Ps. 119.97–104; 2 Tim. 3.14—4.5; Luke 18.1–8

WHEN HE COMES

From the gospel: 'Then Jesus told them a parable about their need to pray always and not to lose heart ... "Yet, when the Son of Man comes, will he find faith on earth?" ' (Luke 18.1, 8b)

The parable of the 'importunate widow' (as the *King James Bible* calls it) underlines the need not only for perseverance in prayer, but also for faith and trust in God to see us through the most severe trial. When Jesus comes back, yes, he will find faith – though perhaps not in every nation; but he will only come when every nation has had a chance to hear the gospel.

We do not know what God plans to do after that, or how many faithful he will find. But his judgement is such that none of the faithful will go unrewarded. God does not deal in miscarriages of justice. The unbelieving judge acceded to the widow's request from the wrong motives. We need to examine our own motives: now is an opportune time, when we can still improve them. If we are uncertain as to the veracity of our motives, Paul advises us to go back to God's word for guidance (2 Tim. 3.16f.).

We can never have enough of it – and it even improves with keeping.

❖ Proper 25 YEAR A

Deut. 34.1–12; Ps. 90.1–6, 13–17; 1 Thess. 2.1–8; Matt. 22.34–46

AGAINST THE ODDS

From the epistle: 'Though we had already suffered and been shamefully maltreated at Philippi, as you know, we had courage in our God to declare to you the gospel of God in spite of great opposition.' (1 Thess. 2.2)

Despite suffering, maltreatment and opposition, Paul had carried on with the work he had been commissioned to do. If we are not opposed, we may well question if we are doing our proper work. Opposition is so often a sign that our mission is going ahead. 'Woe to you when all speak well of you' (Luke 6.26); this is a danger we would do well to avoid!

How high is our confidence threshold? Does it take only a minor incident to deflect us from our purpose? Remember Paul. In another letter he itemizes the hassles he has met in the course of his ministry (2 Cor. 11.23–19). It is a list that takes one's breath away. But God is no respecter of persons: he can ask just as much, if not more, of us.

We can, of course, always opt for an easy ride . . . down the road that's paved with good intentions.

~

Proper 25 YEAR B

Job 42.1–6, 10–17; Ps. 34.1–8, 19–22; Heb. 7.23–28; Mark 10.46–52

RESTORATION

From the Old Testament: 'And the LORD restored the fortunes of Job when he had prayed for his friends; and the LORD gave Job twice as much as he had before.' (Job 42.10)

When Job turned his attention away from his own predicament, to the care of others, things began to improve; when Bartimaeus threw away his beggar's cloak (and thus his meal-ticket), abandoning everything to get to Jesus, he was healed; and because on a certain day a one-off sacrifice was made for us, we have hope of restoration to God's grace, no matter how far away from perfect we have slipped. We can come back to God – but not all the way, for he comes to meet us!

And Job learned that however dire his condition had been, God in his mercy can not only restore, but also double the blessings previously enjoyed.

> Be still, my soul; thy Jesus can repay,
> From his own fulness, all he takes away.
>> (Katharina von Schlegel, 1609–?,
>> tr. Jane Borthwick, 1813–97)

We can reach out for the good things on offer in the world, and for a while enjoy them; but only when we reach out to share what we already have with others, does our condition improve with lasting effect.

~

Proper 25

Joel 2.23–32; Ps. 65; 2 Tim. 4.6–8, 16–18; Luke 18.9–14

NEW HOPE

From the prophets: 'Then afterward I will pour out my spirit on all flesh; your sons and your daughters shall prophesy, your old men shall dream dreams, and your young men shall see visions.' (Joel 2.28)

The outpouring of God's Spirit, for those who do not understand it, has them declaring that the world has been turned upside down (Acts 17.6). What do we make of dreams and visions today? Did God have the ordering of them only in biblical times?

Surely we need to reckon with them now even more, for there are more people in need of the Spirit than ever before; and if he cannot persuade us to listen to him in our frenetically busy days, will he not use the night?

When our young folk get excited for Jesus, do we listen to them, or marginalize them in our worship and prayer groups? Whether we have a large church or a small one, a well-heated or a draughty building, the crucial question is: are we a caring church or not, welcoming all ages, all sorts and conditions of people?

Every person, of every age and background, has a gift of the Spirit for our church. Let's explore our gifts together, and bring new hope and life to our community.

❖ Bible Sunday

Neh. 8.1–4a[5–6], 8–12; Ps. 119.9–16; Col. 3.12–17; Matt. 24.30–35

THE LORD'S JOY

From the Old Testament: 'Then he said to them, "Go your way, eat the fat and drink sweet wine and send portions of them to those for whom nothing is prepared, for this day is holy to our LORD; and do not be grieved, for the joy of the LORD is your strength."' (Neh. 8.10)

Ezra had been reading from the Torah, the 'book of the law of Moses' (v. 1), which had generated such joy among the people that a celebration was called, and the rebuilding of Jerusalem's walls was observed with great festivity, food and presents being shared, and a 'holy day' enjoyed to the full. The people had worked hard, but now their strength was renewed by a God who was in total agreement not only with what they had done, but also with their renewed commitment to keeping his laws. God will always honour commitment in his service, whatever form it takes.

When we accept his word into our minds and hearts, we are given not only spiritual strength, but physical strength: one acts on the other, the spiritual being by far the stronger, able to overcome physical weakness and fatigue (John 4.32). Let us tap much more often into this dynamic source of power, for we need all the strength God can give us in these days.

అ

Bible Sunday   YEAR B

Isa. 55.1–11; Ps. 19.7–14; 2 Tim. 3.14—4.5; John 5.36b–47

INSPIRED BY GOD

From the epistle: 'All scripture is inspired by God, and is useful for teaching, for reproof, for correction, and for training in righteousness, so that everyone who belongs to God may be proficient, equipped for every good work.' (2 Tim. 3.16–17)

It is God's inspiration that sets Scripture apart from other writings; his divine input gives Jesus the authority to promise that the word will outlive even heaven and earth. The more we have of it inside us, the better equipped we shall be to do God's work. Each of us already has much more of the Bible stored in our memory than we imagine. Were we to be incarcerated with no books or access to the media – as was Terry Waite in Beirut – we should find, as did Terry, that a great quantity of God's word was inside us, waiting to be recalled for us by the Holy Spirit (John 14.26).

If we pray the Spirit into action, we need not wait to be taken hostage. He will bring the word up from the recesses of our memories, which are better than all the computers the world has ever had. We never know when we may need to share certain portions of the word: in an emergency, a celebration, a grief, worry, or an accident; but the more of Scripture we have in our hearts, the more we can help when called upon to do so.

It may mean life or death to someone.

Bible Sunday

YEAR C

Isa. 45.22–25; Ps. 119.129–136; Rom. 15.1–6; Luke 4.16–24

ENCOURAGEMENT

From the epistle: 'For whatever was written in former days was written for our instruction, so that by steadfastness and by the encouragement of the scriptures we might have hope.' (Rom. 15.4)

Jesus, who not only had the word of God in him, but who was that Word, read the Scriptures, quoted from them, and taught them. If *he* needed to, how much more do we! Paul and the early apostles also used the Scriptures, together with verbatim reminiscences of Jesus' ministry. We are even more fortunate, having both the Old and New Testaments in more translations and versions than ever before.

So, you think you know a passage? Take a new translation, and let it come alive and fresh to you. Share it with a friend, and benefit from another's insight. Let us carry our Bibles with us; leave Bible verses tucked into the mirror, on the fridge door, taped to the washing machine. By the time we get to heaven, let us be on fire with God's word, and responsible for lighting up as many others with it as possible.

God's word is life. It speaks to every person in every situation. Human nature and needs do not change. Strip away the modern veneer, and you are left with a situation paralleled somewhere in the Bible. Work on it with victory in mind.

❖ Dedication Festival

YEAR A

First Sunday in October or Last Sunday After Trinity

1 Kings 8.22–30 or Rev. 21.9–14; Ps. 122; Heb. 12.18–24; Matt. 21.12–16

GOD'S HOUSE

From the gospel: 'Then Jesus entered the temple and drove out all who were selling and buying in the temple, and he overturned the tables of the money changers and the seats of those who sold doves.' (Matt. 21.12)

It was chaos, with the cages of the sacrificial doves sent awry, and the birds flying free; lambs bleating and wandering here and there; coins clinking across the floor; the sick clamouring to be healed, and children dancing and shouting with excitement. If it happened today, many would complain that 'this is not what the Church is for!'

But the Master was there, in his Father's house. He was not fazed by children being children; and he healed every sick person in need. The entrepreneurs, out to swindle people at their *bureaux de change*, were powerless to retaliate. People were being cured, and children were crowding around Jesus. Nothing like it had happened before.

Today we can reflect on how we are using our churches. Is prayer the number one priority? Does worship come next? Is the bookstall, the coffee annexe, the new meeting-room or the kitchen complementing or distracting from the main purpose of God's house? How can we improve the use and care of our church?

⇛

Dedication Festival

YEAR B

First Sunday in October or Last Sunday After Trinity

Gen. 28.11–18 or Rev. 21.9–14; Ps. 122; 1 Pet. 2.1–10; John 10.22–29

LIVING STONES

From the epistle: 'Come to [the Lord], a living stone, though rejected by mortals yet chosen and precious in God's sight, and like living stones, let yourselves be built into a spiritual house, to be a holy priesthood, to offer spiritual sacrifices acceptable to God through Jesus Christ.' (1 Pet. 2.4–5)

There are two churches: the *physical*, providing a shelter in which the *spiritual* can meet. If we, the spiritual, are not there, the physical is merely a shell, waiting for living souls to arrive and make the worship come alive. Largely, our services are dependent on fairly sedate music and prayers of an earlier time. Even our most modern youth services have but a fraction of the richness of melody and praising in the heavenly courts.

Yet the outward observances, whether staid or stunning, are secondary to the heart-worship we give to God. If we are not worshipping from the heart, why are we there? Stones cannot be incorporated into any building until they have been shaped and fitted into the place chosen for them. Once there, they can fulfil their purpose. We are members of the

Church, come to offer our spiritual sacrifices: worship, praise and thanksgiving; the sharing of God's word, his love and his goodness.

It's an on-going commitment.

❧

Dedication Festival

YEAR C

First Sunday in October or Last Sunday After Trinity

1 Chron. 29.6–19; Ps. 122; Eph. 2.19–22; John 2.13–22

CITIZENS WITH THE SAINTS

From the epistle: 'So then you are no longer strangers and aliens, but you are citizens with the saints and also members of the household of God.' (Eph. 2.19)

We *are* citizens with the saints. We *are* members of the household of God. *Now*. We do not have to wait until we die for citizenship and membership. As we give thanks for those who built our churches, let us also praise God for heaping his grace on us from the time when we first accepted Christ. We do not have to grovel on all fours, begging for a crumb of divine mercy: we come, as full citizens and family members, to feast at the Eucharist. We come as brothers and sisters of Christ, in the house of our (shared) Father.

Or are we so preoccupied with worry, grief or pain, that this joy has passed us by? We have problems, but – large though they may seem – they are nothing compared to the grace God has given us. We meet together to strengthen that grace further; and, if our fellowship means what it should, to share our problems and let grace bear in upon them.

From the times of the tabernacle, or Tent of Meeting, God has given us places in which to worship him. May we use our particular church richly for his glory and the advancement of his kingdom.

❖ All Saints' Day

YEAR A

Rev. 7.9–17; Ps. 34.1–10; 1 John 3.1–3; Matt. 5.1–12

BEFORE THE THRONE

From Revelation: 'After this I looked, and there was a great multitude that no one could count, from every nation, from all tribes and peoples and languages, standing before the throne and before the Lamb, robed in white, with palm branches in their hands.' (Rev. 7.9)

When Pope John Paul II came to England in 1982, he preached to huge crowds, including 350,000 people during an open-air Mass at Coventry airport. The sea of faces stretched about as far as the eye could see. How can one visualize the much greater crowd in the throne-room of heaven – or the dimensions of a room so vast?

It stretches the mind to imagine the 'communion of saints' – yet already we are among them in spirit (Eph. 2.19), and one day we shall be there with them in reality. Each of us, commissioned to share the gospel, is helping to swell the great throng even further – which means we shall be among friends when we arrive in our Father's throne-room.

When circumstances press in upon us here on earth, and threaten to take our minds off God, can we focus in spirit on the saints already there, and those who – like us – are on their way? One day, we shall truly celebrate ALL Saints. *Marana tha*. Even so, come, Lord Jesus.

৵

All Saints' Day   YEAR B

Wisd. 3.1–9 or Isa. 25.6–9; Ps. 24.1–6; Rev. 21.1–6a; John 11.32–44

NEW JERUSALEM

From Revelation: 'Then I saw a new heaven and a new earth; for the first heaven and the first earth had passed away, and the sea was no more. And I saw the holy city, the new Jerusalem, coming down out of heaven from God, prepared as a bride adorned for her husband.' (Rev. 21.1–2)

This is geology on the cosmic scale. God has universe after universe at his command. We cannot visualize infinity, but he is there too. This earth, which seems so vast, and the heaven – which must be so much greater – will both be taken (or thrown) away, to be replaced by a new design. Can we not look at the beauty of the present order, and have faith that God's new Jerusalem will be lovely beyond compare?

The new city will comprise the Church, the Bride of Christ. We shall be there, but our function is not yet clear. God will have new work for us, of that we can be sure: we are not learning how to use his talents here in order to see them wasted when we translate to the next stage.

There will be Anselm, Monica, Boniface, Teresa of Avila, Jerome,

Hildegard of Bingen, John Chrysostom, and all the others whose lives have counted for Christ. What shall we say to them, or they to us?

What a gathering of the ransomed!

❧

All Saints' Day

YEAR C

Dan. 7.1–3, 15–18; Ps. 149; Eph. 1.11–23; Luke 6.20–31

GREAT REWARD

From the gospel: 'Blessed are you when people hate you, and when they exclude you, revile you, and defame you on account of the Son of Man. Rejoice in that day and leap for joy, for surely your reward is great in heaven; for that is what their ancestors did to the prophets.' (Luke 6.22–23)

When opposition comes against us, it is an indication that we are troubling Satan, and thus fulfilling our Christian mission. If we cannot stand the heat, we can cool down to lukewarmness, and no one will bother us. Those who are saints now in glory ran the gauntlet of everything Satan could muster – and won through. Who could descend to becoming lukewarm when we have such an example to follow!

The ranks of heaven's saintly communion are growing by the second. When we join them, life will certainly not be quiet. What we shall be doing is still unknown, but the likelihood is that it will be work connected in some way with that which we have proved to do best here – and that is usually the work we find most congenial.

Memory is a precious gift that is sometimes overlooked – and particularly in times of bereavement, it can be a wounding gift; yet without it we should not appreciate the communion of saints whom we honour today. Praise God for memory!

❖ **The Fourth Sunday Before Advent**   YEAR A

Mic. 3.5–12; Ps. 43; 1 Thess. 2.9–13; Matt. 24.1–14

TELL THE WORLD

From the gospel: 'But the one who endures to the end will be saved. And this good news of the kingdom will be proclaimed throughout the world, as a testimony to all the nations; and then the end will come.' (Matt. 24.13–14)

Implicitly the message is: if you want the end to come (sooner rather than later), envangelize the world. On average, the Bible has been translated into one new language each year of the Christian era. Nearly four thousand languages are still without a complete Bible. Yet today we have technology that would have thrilled St Paul – and vastly more manpower than was at his disposal.

The gospel 'will be proclaimed'. God will get the work done – if not by us, then by others. But as commissioned officers, we are obliged to do what we can: if not to translate, then to pray for translators; if not to take the news to the other side of the world, then to evangelize on the home front; if not to preach, then to teach. We can do it – God has called, and with the call comes the grace.

The saving of souls is God's work: once we have shared the word, we can leave the rest to him. When Jesus' disciples met rejection, they were told to shake off the dust of that town and move to the next.

Can we not sense the urgency of our mission?

ॐ

The Fourth Sunday Before Advent   YEAR B

Deut. 6.1–9; Ps. 119.1–8; Heb. 9.11–14; Mark 12.28–34

HOW MUCH MORE!

From the epistle: 'For if the blood of goats and bulls, with the sprinkling of the ashes of a heifer, sanctifies those who have been defiled so that their flesh is purified, how much more will the blood of Christ, who through the eternal Spirit offered himself without blemish to God, purify our conscience from dead works to worship the living God!' (Heb. 9.13–14)

We can imagine something of the relief and new courage experienced by Israelites after each Day of Atonement. Cleansed from the past year's sin, they were able once more to start over, with the record wiped clean. The blood of innocent animals had shown to God man's intention to repent. Innocence had cancelled out guilt.

So it was at Calvary, but on a grander scale. This time, God died; man could not have the physical satisfaction of offering a sacrifice; he needed to believe his purification had been freely effected. How much more difficult this is to accept!

If Calvary does not shame us into accepting Jesus' sacrifice, we are clinging to sin that God has already negated. He is a Gentleman. He will not forcibly deprive us of our guilt. He has taken the sin and dropped it into the sea of his love.

Yet if we want to waste the time, we can always go fishing to reclaim it.

&

The Fourth Sunday Before Advent   YEAR C

Isa. 1.10–18; Ps. 32.1–7; 2 Thess. 1.1–12; Luke 19.1–10

I WILL PAY BACK

From the gospel: 'Zacchaeus stood there and said to the Lord, "Look, half of my possessions, Lord, I will give to the poor; and if I have defrauded anyone of anything, I will pay back four times as much."' (Luke 19.8)

A receptionist was agreeably amazed when her employer's client handed back an extra pound coin she had been given in the change for a consultancy fee. The world today generally does not expect honesty. Let us, as Christians, keep shocking it by keeping honest-dealing as our hallmark. Zacchaeus would no doubt startle his guests by his declaration of future honesty. 'Why bother, if you can get away with it?' is not exclusively a modern method.

When Jesus comes close, he highlights any dark corners in our lives, until we have attended to their thorough spring-cleaning. The process may hurt, but any damage will not be permanent. To live as those who may one day die, means learning to live light to many pieces of baggage we hitherto considered essential.

Salvation comes to Zacchaeus' house, in the form of Christ himself; but Jesus would have left, with the house unsaved, had not Zacchaeus met him halfway, and responded to the goodness that he recognized.

❖ The Third Sunday Before Advent YEAR A

Wisd. 6.12–16 or Amos 5.18–24; *Canticle*: Wisd. 6.17–20 or Ps. 70; 1 Thess. 4.13–18; Matt. 25.1–13

TRUE WISDOM

From the apocrypha: 'The beginning of wisdom is the most sincere desire for instruction, . . . so the desire for wisdom leads to a kingdom.' (Wisd. 6.17a, 20)

Instruction, love, obedience, immortality: proceed up these four steps, says the author of Wisdom, and they will lead you to God and his kingdom. The first three steps are earthly, the last, heavenly. Where on this ladder of life are we? Perhaps with one foot on the first rung, and the other on the second. So long as we are on the ladder somewhere, we are heading towards God.

Heaven is not reached in a single leap, nor by those who have decided they need no further instruction; nor by those who have little love for themselves or others; nor yet by those who put their ways and wishes before those of God.

Whether it is Emmaus, Alpha, Cursillo, or any local variation, every parish needs Bible study groups for its on-going spiritual instruction, as back-up for Sunday preaching. It is noticeable that in areas where the Church is experiencing rapid and sustained growth (as in many parts of China and Africa), there are many such groups meeting – and filling their halls and homes to capacity – on practically every weekday evening.

A Church that is constantly seeking instruction is an exploratory, open-hearted Church.

᷊

The Third Sunday Before Advent   YEAR B

Jonah 3.1–5, 10; Ps. 62.5–12; Heb. 9.24–28; Mark 1.14–20

GOD CHANGED HIS MIND

From the prophets: 'Jonah began to go into the city, going a day's walk.
And he cried out, "Forty days more, and Nineveh shall be overthrown!"
... When God saw what they did, how they turned from their evil ways,
God changed his mind about the calamity ... and he did not do it.'
(Jonah 3.4, 10)

It is almost incredible that our repentance can cause God to change his
mind; but intercession for others can have a similar effect (as when
Abraham pleaded for the Sodomites); or persistence in prayer (as in the
case of the importunate widow). God has a loving heart, open to
pleading, sensitive to our fears and feelings. Were it otherwise, should
we ever have the heart to pray?

God is not to be manipulated, but neither is he unmovable. Jonah
could not understand this. He could pray to God for himself, but his
theology faltered when others for whom he had no love were recipients
of God's mercy. There are enough Jonahs in the modern world, without
us swelling their ranks.

Have you got a problem that is too big for God? Then you are a
walking phenomenon, no longer of the human race, with no business
taking up space on the earth!

Let us have boldness to come to God in prayer, knowing that he will
weigh our words, and will answer accordingly.

Yes, truly, he *will* answer, every time.

ॐ

The Third Sunday Before Advent   YEAR C

Job 19.23–27a; Ps. 17.1–9; 2 Thess. 2.1–5, 13–17; Luke 20.27–38

AS GOD SEES US

From the gospel: 'Now he is God not of the dead, but of the living; for to
him all of them are alive.' (Luke 20.38)

How do you see yourself today? Joyful or sad? Fulfilled or dissatisfied?
Healthy or sick? Peaceful or worried? But how do you think God sees
you?

We mourn the loss of a loved one and weep at the grave. But God does not see that person as dead: he or she is living, more vibrantly and fully than ever before. Could we but see with God's vision, we should not look to the graveyard as the 'dead centre' of the parish – but instead to the church as its 'living heart' – a place, a community, where those in the Nearer Presence are exactly that: closer to present-day believers than ever they were in 'life'. Their influence and worth has not gone with their bodies to the grave. To God, *all* of us are alive.

Perhaps we would grieve less if we reflected more on these words of Jesus. If we have been left for a time on our own, then God knows we can cope: he never calls us to do or endure anything beyond our capabilities. The sooner we adapt to any new situation, and make of it something beautiful for God, the wider we are opening the door for him to move us on to the next stage in our spiritual development. Our view is two-dimensional: God's view adds the future to the past and present.

❖ **The Second Sunday Before Advent** YEAR A

Zeph. 1.7, 12–18; Ps. 90.1–8[9–11], 12; 1 Thess. 5.1–11; Matt. 25.14–30

BE A FRIEND

From the epistle: 'Therefore encourage one another and build up each other, as indeed you are doing.' (1 Thess. 5.11)

It is impossible to be a friendless Christian, for our commission is to love one another; and love encourages and builds up the one to whom it is shown. If we look for defects in a friend, we shall find them – and we may very well lose our friend. But if we look for good qualities, we shall also find those; and affirming them, and encouraging their use and growth in Christian service, will deepen the friendship – and almost certainly expand into reciprocal affirmation.

We love to be loved – and the Lord, when he made us that way, was mirroring his own loving nature. In its simplest terms, it means putting others before ourselves: if they have a little gift or aptitude, we can show appreciation, and the gift will grow. If they have already moved mountains in the exercising of their gift, our affirmation and encouragement may see them go from strength to strength and move continents!

But, yes, we get it wrong at times. Who hasn't seen the hurt in a friend's eyes, and realized that – however well intentioned – our words have come as a snub, or a disappointment?

Let us today take the Thessalonians' example to heart, and see how we can win more friends for Christ.

෪

The Second Sunday Before Advent YEAR B

Dan. 12.1–3; Ps. 16; Heb. 10.11–14[15–18], 19–25; Mark 13.1–8

SHINING AS STARS

From the prophets: 'Those who are wise shall shine like the brightness of the sky, and those who lead many to righteousness, like the stars forever and ever.' (Dan. 12.3)

A verse like this is surely an encouragement to us, to work ever harder to evangelize the world, that the end may come sooner rather than later (Matt. 24.14; Mark 13.10).

We belong to the Church of 6,000 languages (two-thirds of which have still to be realized); to the Church of many nations (two-thirds of whom have yet to hear the gospel); to the worldwide mission-field of God, where the harvest is still not gathered in. Evangelism should be our number one priority.

The little pinpricks of light that flicker brightest on a moonless night, and are still there but unnoticed in the day, rarely impact on a society that now uses more down-to-earth navigation. Yet stars are often mentioned in the Bible. 'Where were you,' God asked Job, 'when the morning stars sang together?' And Jesus himself is called 'the bright and morning star'. Can we grasp that one day we shall shine like the stars? We are currently being prepared for such honour. Can we grasp this too?

Today, while the world careens about us, can we focus on the truth that the Christian's life here should be 'from glory to glory advancing'?

෪

The Second Sunday Before Advent

Mal. 4.1–2a; Ps. 98; 2 Thess. 3.6–13; Luke 21.5–19

TO GIVE AN EXAMPLE

From the epistle: 'We did not eat anyone's bread without paying for it; but with toil and labor we worked night and day, so that we might not burden any of you. This was not because we do not have that right, but in order to give you an example to imitate.' (2 Thess. 3.8–9)

Paul would know as well as anyone that the labourer is worthy of his hire. He makes this clear to the Thessalonians; but in order to teach them the value of going the second mile, he not only preaches the gospel full time, but supports himself as well. These new Christians can see him and his mission-team relying on no one for their subsistence. Thessalonica was proud of its culture as well as its trade. Money, success and self-sufficiency were writ large in the city's charter. Paul had astutely devined that for a visiting mission-team to be dependent on charity would not make the best impact.

Can we be as flexible in our ministry? Can we read a parish, a community, and 'be all things to all'? Can we exercise our ministry – not compromising the gospel, but also being careful not to present the gospel or ourselves in such a way that people will mistake it, or us, for someone other than Jesus?

Jesus warns us that those who are bent on hating us will (Luke 21.17). That is their problem. Let us be faithful.

❖ Christ the King

Ezek. 34.11–16, 20–24; Ps. 95.1–7a; Eph. 1.15–23; Matt. 25.31–46

JUST AS YOU DID IT TO ME

From the gospel: 'Then the righteous will answer him, "Lord, when was it that we saw you hungry and gave you food, or thirsty and gave you something to drink?" ... "Truly I tell you, just as you did it to one of the least of these who are members of my family, you did it to me."' (Matt. 25.37, 40b)

With God, nothing is trivial. The time he gives us is precious, every second of it; and we are constantly being given opportunities to be used in time, for eternity. To us, some of these opportunities may seem small and insignificant; but if we are always waiting for the spectacular mission, and conserving our abundant energies and talents merely for the mega-works, we stand in danger of letting a host of equally important, if less high-profile, opportunities be snapped up by someone else.

We need to grasp every opportunity for service that God gives us, for it may be the last before we go to glory. Eternity is a long time to regret even one missed chance. A life – or even a day – packed with little kindnesses is preferable to chronic spiritual inertia cultivated by waiting for the big opportunity that always went to someone else.

We are not someone else's keeper: we have a soul to save for eternity, which God knows by our name and no one else's.

જે

Christic the King YEAR B

Dan. 7.9–10, 13–14; Ps. 93; Rev. 1.4b–8; John 18.33–37

SO YOU ARE A KING?

From the gospel: 'Pilate asked him, "So you are a king?" Jesus answered, "You say that I am a king. For this I was born, and for this I came into the world, to testify to the truth."' (John 18.37a–b)

John in his Gospel emphasizes Pilate's dealing with Jesus as a king. He would hang on the cross under a kingly titulus. Pilate would cleverly trap the Jews into declaring allegiance to another 'king', Caesar; but, protest as they might, the same Jews would see their true King at Calvary.

'You are a king?' Whether we phrase it as a question or a statement, Christ still reigns today: from the cross, for those who have yet to repent and be healed by his blood; and from the throne for those who are already his. He is either the Lord of glory, Alpha and Omega – or he is rejected and blasphemed. But he is still a King, as those who reject and blaspheme him will one day discover.

Jesus will not impose his authority before the End of the world. He could have convinced Pilate beyond all doubt; but the Roman had a responsibility to believe for himself, as we all have.

Jesus was born to be a king, because from the alpha-beginning of the world that is what he was. Few believed his testimony, because he chose to veil his majesty. But now his secret is out. We can tell it to whom we wish. And a modern Pilate will always ask: 'And is it true?'

≈

Christer the King   YEAR C

Jer. 23.1–6; Ps. 46; Col. 1.11–20; Luke 23.33–43

JESUS, REMEMBER ME

From the gospel: 'Then he said, "Jesus, remember me when you come into your kingdom!"' (Luke 23.42)

The ecclesiastical hierarchy had rejected their King, but the penitent thief acknowledged Jesus' royal status. Had he read Pilate's notice? Or had he heard of Jesus and his ministry? Or did God give this wretched man a sudden, wonderful, life-giving revelation, as he hung in agony? We do not know. But the man's brave confession of faith called forth a promise that has given comfort to millions since: 'Today you will be with me in Paradise.'

Where this 'beautiful garden' is, we need not know. One day we shall be there, within perhaps a split second of our death. The various ancient texts have no problem with 'today': we can believe it as it stands. There will be no protracted time in purgatory or limbo.

Throughout Jesus' ministry, we hear of demons recognizing our Lord, while his own people, notably the theologians of his day, rejected him. And at Calvary, it takes a Roman to write his regal notice, and a thief to recognize and affirm his royalty.

Doesn't this say something about the danger of preconceived ideas? But such ideas are not part of *our* make-up, are they?

MAJOR SAINTS' DAYS

❖ **The Naming and Circumcision of Jesus**   1 January

Num. 6.22–27; Ps. 8; Gal. 4.4–7; Luke 2.15–21

ACCORDING TO CUSTOM

From the gospel: 'After eight days had passed, it was time to circumcise the child; and he was called Jesus, the name given by the angel before he was conceived in the womb.' (Luke 2.21)

Names are important. They set us apart as special people. Jesus calls every one of his sheep by name. Jeremiah was told that God knew him before he was formed in the womb, and so we should not be surprised that Jesus was named prior to his conception. When John the Baptist was circumcised, his naming saw the miraculous restoration of Zechariah's speech.

Usually our name is decided for us at birth or baptism, by parents and godparents. We may change it when we reach adulthood, but generally it is simpler to let it stay with us. Other people use our name more than we do ourselves, though we may write or type it quite often. Usually it is spoken by friends, in love – as Jesus used Peter's, Martha's, and Mary's names. If we had to describe what a friend's name means to us, we should concentrate on things like love, happiness, friendship, loyalty – rather than our friend's clothes, choice of lipstick, house or car.

So, names encapsulate the parts of a person that really matter. Surely that is why 'Jesus' means simply 'Saviour'.

❖ **The Conversion of Paul**   25 January

Jer. 1.4–10; Ps. 67; Acts 9.1–22 or Gal. 1.11–16a; Matt. 19.27–30

NOT AN EARTHLY COMMAND

From the epistle: 'I want you to know, brothers and sisters, that the gospel that was proclaimed by me is not of human origin; for I did not receive it from a human source, nor was I taught it, but I received it through a revelation of Jesus Christ.' (Gal. 1.11–12)

The 'Damascus road experience' changed the Church's most ardent persecutor into its most ardent apostle. Few, if any, of us have had such a dramatic conversion, so we cannot fully appreciate the impact it must have had on Paul – or what the growth of the early Church would have been like had the conversion not taken place.

Rabbi Li'ezer ben Jacob used to say: 'Repentance and good works are as a shield against punishment' (*Pirke Aboth*, 4.15); and Paul's post-conversion life is an example of what one man whose mind is set on good works can do to turn around a life that has been heading in exactly the opposite direction.

Paul's trust in the redeeming power of Christ to blot out his sins was such that he could say that he now had nothing of which to be ashamed.

It is a lesson to us to repent of sin, *and then to let it go:* to go forward in confidence that God has erased it from our record, washing clean our page in his Book of Life, in the blood of Jesus.

❖ Timothy and Titus   26 January

Isa. 61.1–3a; Ps. 100; 2 Tim. 2.1–8 or Titus 1.1–5; Luke 10.1–9

MY GOSPEL – OUR FAITH

From the epistles: 'Remember Jesus Christ, raised from the dead, a descendant of David – that is my gospel.' (2 Tim. 2.8)

'To Titus, my loyal child in the faith we share.' (Titus 1.4a)

Paul – perhaps after the unfortunate disagreement over Mark's loyalty – grew to be tolerant and loving towards younger ministers in the faith. He is generous with his advice, patient in his counselling. He wants them to come to know his gospel as he knows and loves it: to share the faith that has seen him through so much.

This joint commemoration of Timothy and Titus is a time to reflect on our own outreach to young Christians, and aspiring Christians. Do we welcome them to our worship and witness as much as we could? Do we encourage them to participate fully in the life of our church? Do we listen to them, as much as we hope they will listen to us?

They are brimful of ideas, these young people. Can we share their visions, their enthusiasm, their commitment? Can we show them we have not (yet) got all the answers (though we're working on it)? Paul wrote the second letter to Timothy when he was under house-arrest in Rome, waiting to make his defence to Nero. By this time, Timothy had been consecrated as the first Bishop of Ephesus.

Perhaps we have a future bishop among our young worshippers.

❖ Joseph

19 March

2 Sam. 7.4–16; Ps. 89.27–36; Rom. 4.13–18; Matt. 1.18–25

THINGS YET TO BE

From the epistle: 'But also to those who share the faith of Abraham ... in the presence of the God in whom he believed, who gives life to the dead and calls into existence the things that do not exist.' (Rom. 4.16b–17)

Joseph had to take everything on trust: a miraculous conception and all that this entailed; the gossip of neighbours; the sheer impossibility if it were all true; the question of Mary's propriety if it were not. And yet this man, who so remarkably and with such quiet dignity put such trust in God, speaks not a single word in the New Testament! By the time Jesus begins his ministry, Joseph has faded from the scene, presumed dead: a father who physically had played no part in the conception of his son.

Yet from Jesus' religious observance (Luke 4.16), we can assume that Joseph was a devout, churchgoing man; and the Christian Church for centuries has honoured the quiet carpenter on this day. We, too, may not make headline news; we may not hold people spellbound with oratory. But, just as God involved Joseph so intimately in his salvation plan, may we also be prepared to accept any opportunity he may give us, with the quiet confidence and dignity shown by Joseph.

❖ The Annunciation 25 March

Isa. 7.10–14; Ps. 40.5–10; Heb. 10.4–10; Luke 1.26–38

AS GOD WILLS

From the prophets: 'Therefore the Lord himself will give you a sign. Look, the young woman is with child and shall bear a son, and shall name him Immanuel.' (Isa. 7.14)

It was not Ahaz's lack of confidence regarding a sign that angered God, but the king's refusal to obey a divine order. God decided for him, and so we have the promise that came so wonderfully true around eight centuries later.

'Ask of me, and I will give it.' This command of God is found in many parts of scripture. Gideon asked for two signs, and both were given. And today, when we 'put out a fleece', God often honours our plea and gives us confidence to move on in faith.

But Jesus, though he gave many miraculous signs, warned us against asking when we already have the answer, or perhaps a clue to the answer (Matt. 12.39f.). Mary did not seek her sign: it was brought to her in an astounding way.

God does not ask us to navigate our spiritual journey without signs, though the majority of us probably miss them most of the time. Let us be cautious against asking for a sign when our way ahead is clear; but, when God appears to be telling us to consult him about a course of action, or actually presenting us with a sign, let us have the quiet confidence of Mary rather than the unwillingness of Ahaz.

❖ George, Patron Saint of England 23 April

1 Macc. 2.59–64 or Rev. 12.7–12; Ps. 126; 2 Tim. 2.3–13; John 15.18–21

FAITHFUL, TRUE AND LOYAL

From the apocrypha: 'My children, be courageous and grow strong in the law, for by it you will gain honour.' (1 Macc. 2.64)

The legends of St George are numerous, too many for an accurate life history to be gleaned with confidence. He appears to have been a knight of Cappadocia, who killed a man-eating beast at the Libyan city of

Sylene, and subsequently converted the citizens to Christianity. He was martyred around AD 303 in Palestine.

Faithfulness, truth, loyalty and courage are estimable virtues, and characterize those who through the years have made their stand for Christ, often against severe odds. In honouring George today, we can also honour our country whose patron saint he has been for so long. Bad news may crowd the headlines, but England has still much that is green and pleasant: those who still put Christ before all else – showing a faithfulness, truth, loyalty and courage akin to that of George – and who are proud today to attend patronal services and to show the flag of St George.

Many are critical of patriotism today; but when this loyalty is linked to Christian patriotism, it transcends the merely national sphere – for, like George, our true citizenship is in heaven (Eph. 2.19).

❖ Mark   25 April

Prov. 15.28–33 or Acts 15.35–41; Ps. 119.9–16; Eph. 4.7–16; Mark 13.5–13

BUILDERS FOR CHRIST

From the epistle: 'The gifts [Christ] gave were that some would be apostles, some prophets, some evangelists, some pastors and teachers, to equip the saints for the work of ministry, for building up the body of Christ.' (Eph. 4.11–12)

Mark's Gospel, the earliest of our canonical Gospels, starkly sets out the message and impact of Jesus. Salvation is freely offered, but the cost of discipleship is high: we shall be misunderstood, misrepresented and hated; we may be called upon to suffer loss and pain. However, the few who bear up under this pressure will be amply repaid.

Mark joined Paul on his mission until a dispute saw the team split into two, with Barnabas taking Mark while Paul commissioned Silas to accompany him on his second journey. Later, however, Mark was with Paul during the apostle's imprisonment in Rome. Since Mark is recorded by Papias, Bishop of Hierapolis, as being an 'interpreter' of Peter, we may indeed be justified in recognizing a virtual eyewitness freshness and detail in his recording of the events of Jesus' ministry.

Christ is still equipping 'saints' for the work of ministry. We may have another Mark in our midst even now, being prepared to share the good news of the gospel – perhaps by translating it into one of the 4,000 languages still without a Bible.

❖ Philip and James   1 May

Isa. 30.15–21; Ps. 119.1–8; Eph. 1.3–10; John 14.1–14

PLAN FOR THE FUTURE

From the epistle: 'With all wisdom and insight he has made known to us the mystery of his will, according to his good pleasure that he set forth in Christ, as a plan for the fulness of time, to gather up all things in him, things in heaven and things on earth.' (Eph. 1.8–10)

Only God can hold in place the countless lives that contribute to his master-plan. We may feel our particular part is so small as to be unimportant; but nothing is trivial with God. Jesus called 12 men to be his 'A' team for mission: some, like Peter and James and John, had a high profile; one is remembered for doubting, another for betraying him; others, like Philip and James ('the Less'), rate only an occasional mention in the Gospels, and virtually nothing is known of their subsequent ministry. Yet they are no less vital to God's plan.

Philip introduced Nathanael to Jesus; he was tested before the miraculous feeding; and his question received the beautiful teaching of Jesus in John 14. James was the son of Alphaeus, and may also have been at Calvary (Mark 15.40). Since 1 May AD 560, the Church has linked their celebrations, which saw the dedication of the church in Rome that houses their remains.

Each day our ministry is being dovetailed into God's plan – regardless of whether or not it is making the world's headlines.

❖ Matthias

Isa. 22.15–25 or Acts 1.15–26; Ps. 15; 1 Cor. 4.1–7; John 15.9–17

A TRUSTY STEWARD

From the epistle: 'Think of us in this way, as servants of Christ and stewards of God's mysteries. Moreover, it is required of stewards that they be found trustworthy.' (1 Cor. 4.1–2)

Matthias does not figure large in the New Testament. He and Joseph Barsabas were the candidates nominated for election to replace Judas Iscariot in the number of the Twelve. The lot fell to Matthias, whom Peter acknowledged as having been with Jesus' mission-team from its inception, and who had also witnessed his resurrection.

It was a good recommendation. Matthias had not sought high position or honour, but had proved loyal and trustworthy in his quiet allegiance to the cause. He is thought to have written a gospel, which is quoted by some early writers, but nothing else is known of his ministry.

We are 'servants', 'stewards' of God's purpose, Paul tells us; and all that is required of us is faithfulness. It can be hard to carry on when others are moving mountains, or when our motives are impugned, or when grief, worry or pain tries to immobilize not only our bodies but also our minds. But if we are faithful, we shall ride out the storm. It will pass.

❖ The Visit of Mary to Elizabeth

Zeph. 3.14–18; Ps. 113; Rom. 12.9–16; Luke 1.39–49[50–56]

SHARE GOOD NEWS

From the gospel: 'In those days Mary set out and went with haste to a Judean town in the hill country, where she entered the house of Zechariah and greeted Elizabeth.' (Luke 1.39–40)

Good news is meant to be shared. Mary left behind everything to spend three months with Elizabeth. Jesus left behind glory to come and tell the world it had a chance. Peter and the others left home, family and employment to spread the news.

We may not personally evangelize the world in our lifetime, but we are leaving the next generation a legacy on which to build. Do we share everything God has given us, with the generosity he has shown?

We have become proficient in sharing worry and pain and grief:
society bristles with counsellors and practitioners for all of these.
But are we as quick to share joys and the best of good news?

The angels shared good news with the shepherds, on the very night
of Jesus' birth; and with Mary and the others on the day of Jesus'
resurrection. Let us not become so conditioned to the world's pre-
occupation with negative news that we forget even a smile can lift
another's spirits – or a cup of tea, a bunch of flowers, or just a hug.

❖ Barnabas   11 June

Job 29.11–16 or Acts 11.19–30; Ps. 112; Gal. 2.1–10; John 15.12–17

A GOOD TEACHER

From the epistle: 'Then Barnabas went to Tarsus to look for Saul, and
when he had found him, he brought him to Antioch. So it was that for
an entire year they met with the church and taught a great many people,
and it was in Antioch that the disciples were first called "Christians." '(Acts 11.25–26)

Barnabas is noted for his courage, insight and missionary expertise as
well as his proficiency in PR. He supported the veracity of Paul's
conversion, and stayed loyal to Mark despite Paul's reservations. He
was a good man to have at one's side when the locals turned nasty; and
when the Lycaonians fêted the apostles as gods, Barnabas was not
carried away by the lure of worldly honour.

These are qualities needed just as vitally by the Church today. Jesus
warned us that the most insidious danger can be the pull of the world.
Little by little, leisure, glitz and problems draw us away from concen-
tration on God; and a marginalized faith is next-door to no faith at all.

Even Paul, who was an exceptionally forceful character, acquiesced
when Barnabas stood up for Mark – and the result was two mission-
teams instead of one. We may not always be able to avoid confrontations
in our churches, but let us pray that these may give rise to vital blessings.

❖ The Birth of John the Baptist 24 June

Isa. 40.1–11; Ps. 85.7–13; Acts 13.14b–26 or Gal. 3.23–29; Luke 1.57–66, 80

PREPARATION FOR MINISTRY

From the gospel: 'The child grew and became strong in spirit, and he was in the wilderness until the day he appeared publicly to Israel.' (Luke 1.80)

Did John, in those 30 years or so of wilderness 'exile', ever feel his wonderful talent for preaching was being wasted? It can often be much more difficult to have our worth laid aside for a while than to be scurrying around in God's service, trying to fit two days into one. 'Lord, you've given me such a gift, and I'm not using it!' If the fault lies with us, fair enough: we can surely do something to right it. But if, after all we've tried, we are still prevented from using that gift, do we become fretful or resentful – or instead accept that God in his wisdom might be giving us a breathing-space?

Perhaps John was made to realize that he would be told when and where to move. Perhaps he did chafe at the seeming waste of time, out there in the desert. Perhaps it was his earlier frustration that gave the edge to his urgent preaching, and made him undiplomatically caustic. God had led John to a place where he could preach his message without fear or favour.

Has God stirred us up in this way? Or are we still learning as he keeps us in the wilderness of his preparation time?

❖ Peter and Paul 29 June

Zech. 4.1–6a, 10b–14 or Acts 12.1–11; Ps. 125; 2 Tim. 4.6–8, 17–18; Matt. 16.13–19

GIVEN STRENGTH

From the epistle: 'But the Lord stood by me and gave me strength, so that through me the message might be fully proclaimed and all the Gentiles might hear it. So I was rescued from the lion's mouth.' (2 Tim. 4.17)

Surely these two, Peter and Paul, are the heavyweights of the early Church! Yet here is one of them saying simply that he did what he did because a greater presence than he stood by him and gave him whatever strength he needed. 'Not to us, Lord, but to you, be the glory.' Whatever we do, in God's name, we do in his strength, not our own. We have no spiritual strength. We are as sheep. All we have is from the indwelling power of God. We are his instruments, honed and sharpened for the work he calls us to do. Peter, as well as Paul, knew this (1 Pet. 1.5).

We may do great things for God – but unless we give him all the credit, they become merely an ego trip. God will use us to show himself to others. We shall not see him in us, but they will. From frescoes and paintings, and the scanty descriptions of contemporary writers, we can, if we want, build up a reasonably accurate picture of Peter and Paul.

But they would not wish it.

May the work we do, and the people we are, similarly make more impact on others than how we appear.

❖ Thomas   3 July

Hab. 2.1–4; Ps. 31.1–6; Eph. 2.19–22; John 20.24–29

WAIT FOR IT

From the prophets: 'For there is still a vision for the appointed time; it speaks of the end, and does not lie. If it seems to tarry, wait for it; it will surely come, it will not delay.' (Hab. 2.3)

Thomas had to learn to wait for God's timing. When Jesus went to Bethany, Thomas believed he was wrong. Lazarus was dead, and Bethany could be dangerous (John 11.16). And, most significantly, Thomas was slow to believe that the resurrection had taken place, though one short week later his doubts were convincingly overcome.

He is thought to have gone to India as a missionary after Christ's ascension. His 'vision', though it had seemed to tarry, had come, and the effects of it were lasting (John 20.28).

We may have to wait longer than a week for God to make real what he has promised. Abraham waited 25 years for Isaac. His mother Monica prayed 22 years for the conversion of Augustine of Hippo. God will not be timed by our chronology or wishes, but he will honour his promises.

Every one.

❖ Mary Magdalene 22 July

Song of Sol. 3.1–4; Ps. 42.1–7; 2 Cor. 5.14–17; John 20.1–2, 11–18

LOVE OF CHRIST

From the epistle: 'For the love of Christ urges us on, … From now on, therefore, we regard no one from a human point of view.' (2 Cor. 5.14a, 16a)

It is thought that Mary of Magdala was a prostitute before Jesus healed her. If so, many with long memories for scandal would be shocked that the person given the honour of being the first to see Jesus resurrected was Mary! But God does not keep a record of repented sin, and as Christians we are warned against judging and assessing on purely human grounds.

Her love for Jesus urged Mary to Calvary, and then to the tomb. What did it matter if people commented or sneered? And God rewarded her loyalty. Our memories are a precious gift from God, but it must grieve him when we keep them sharp by the recollection of things that should be forgotten.

How much does the love of Christ urge us on? Is it more important to us than what people say or do? Does it encourage us to do more than convention requires? Is it the overriding factor in our daily life – or just on one day in every seven?

If we are convinced that Jesus died for all, then nothing is impossible.

❖ James 25 July

Jer. 45.1–5; Ps. 126; Acts 11.27—12.2 or 2 Cor. 4.7–15; Matt. 20.20–28

CALLED TO GLORY

From the Acts: 'About that time King Herod laid violent hands upon some who belonged to the church. He had James, the brother of John, killed with the sword.' (Acts 12.1–2)

Herod Agrippa I was the son of Aristobulus and the grandson of Herod the Great and Mariamne. By martyring James, he hoped to deal the Jerusalem Church a mortal blow; but, as Tertullian was later to write, 'The blood of the martyrs is seed', and the seeds of worldwide mission had already been sown in the life of James. Brother of John, called from the fishing of Galilee to fish for men, he may have had over-eager aspirations for honour (or his mother had, on his behalf: Mark 10.35; Matt. 20.20); but James was loyal – and he was privileged to witness Christ's transfiguration, his agony and the post-resurrection appearances. That he was remarkably brave is seen in his acceptance of high office in the Jerusalem Church, for Jerusalem at that time was no health resort for declared followers of Jesus.

We may not be called to wear a martyr's crown, but every day we need to make choices of one kind or another – some of which may be difficult, others easy, and many pleasurable. May God, as we reflect on the courage of James in his choices, grant us also bravery as we face our lesser Calvaries.

❖ Anne and Joachim 26 July

Zeph. 4.14–17; Ps. 127; Rom. 8.28–30; Matt. 13.16–17

WORKING FOR GOOD

From the epistle: 'We know that all things work together for good for those who love God, who are called according to his purpose.' (Rom. 8.28)

Tradition tells us the names of the parents of the Blessed Virgin Mary, and of how they waited and prayed for many years before God gave them a child. We may reflect on other long-delayed births, such as Abraham's and Sarah's, Hannah's and Elizabeth's – and of how Isaac, Samuel and John the Baptist grew to make spiritual history.

Why does God test the patience and loyalty of those who seem most crucial to his plans? Jesus likened us to the vines with the best promise, which the vine-dresser pruned and trained and fed more thoroughly than the also-rans. If we are being thus dealt with, let us take heart that God is preparing us for something he alone knows is possible. No one has yet realized his own spiritual potential.

If we believe Mary was a very special person, even before the visit of Gabriel, we can surely believe her parents were also highly favoured by God. That we know so little of them is immaterial. We shall meet them one day, and the whole story may be told.

❖ Mary, Martha and Lazarus

Isa. 25.6–9; Ps. 49.5–10, 16; Heb. 2.10–15; John 12.1–8

A LOVING HOME

From the gospel: 'Six days before the Passover Jesus came to Bethany, the home of Lazarus, whom he had raised from the dead. There they gave a dinner for him. Martha served, and Lazarus was one of those at the table with him.' (John 12.1–2)

Mary, Jesus' mother, seems to have given up her home life to travel with him in the mission-team; and this family at Bethany appears to be the nearest approach to a home that Jesus knew during his ministry. Lazarus had been raised from the dead, Mary had been commended for her love and attention to his teaching, and Martha had been commended for her recognition of Jesus as the Messiah. Jesus loved all three, and his love was generously repaid.

With all the antipathy and venom from much of the ecclesiastical hierarchy of the time, it is good to know that Jesus had good friends with whom he could relax and enjoy fellowship. As we reflect on the pleasure given and received at the home in Bethany, let us thank God for all that friendships mean to us.

Can we be friends with those who ask much or little of us? With those who may, or may not, value our friendship? With all whom God brings into our lives in some way or another?

In order to have a friend, we need to be one.

❖ The Transfiguration

Dan. 7.9–10, 13–14; Ps. 97; 2 Pet. 1.16–19; Luke 9.28–36

MAJESTIC GLORY

From the epistle: 'For [Jesus] received honour and glory from God the Father when that voice was conveyed to him by the Majestic Glory, saying, "This is my Son, my Beloved, with whom I am well pleased."' (1 Pet. 1.17)

In the transfiguration, God opened a window of heaven. We do not know the full brightness, the extent of the Majestic Glory, or what we shall be doing – only that it will be 'good for us' to be there (Luke 9.33).

Can we trust God so far? If so, we can also trust that those who have gone before us will be there – recognizable, loving, conversing as they used to do. God is consistent: in the transfiguration, we can believe everything – or nothing; and if we believe nothing, we shall not be there anyway.

God continues to give us glimpses of heaven, at the times of his choosing. Have you, for instance, noticed that a rainbow does not shine after every shower, or that sometimes we see it when someone else has had the rain? Have you experienced a disheartening anti-climax to something that you had looked forward to for a long time, yet been delightfully surprised when something you had dreaded turned out to be really lovely?

Let God be God, and continue to surprise us in his love.

❖ The Assumption of the Blessed Virgin Mary   15 August

Isa. 61.10–11 or Rev. 11.19—12.6, 10; Ps. 45.10–17; Gal. 4.4–7; Luke 1.46–55

FULNESS OF TIME

From the epistle: 'But when the fulness of time had come, God sent his Son, born of a woman, born under the law, in order to redeem those who were under the law, so that we might receive adoption as children.' (Gal. 4.4–5)

The last time we see Mary in the New Testament is after the ascension, when she was with the disciples and 'certain women', devoting themselves to prayer in anticipation of the coming of the Holy Spirit (Acts 1.14).

Traditions vary after this, the Eastern (Orthodox) Church accepting her death and burial, the Western (Catholic) Church believing in her bodily assumption into heaven. If we know and love Mary in our hearts, rejoicing that she is reunited with her Son, perhaps it does not matter overmuch as to how she got there. It is possible – even probable – that Jesus did not allow the body of one who was so special to him to see corruption; but however Mary's earthly life ended, we can today reflect on the importance of how that life was lived.

And while we revere her,
Chaste Mother and Maid,
Do Thou, Jesus, hear her,
And lend us Your aid.

(The Venerable Bede, tr.)

❖ Bartholomew 24 August

Isa. 43.8–13 or Acts 5.12–16; Ps. 145.1–7; 1 Cor. 4.9–15; Luke 22.24–30

FIRM IN TRIALS

From the gospel: 'You are those who have stood by me in my trials; and I confer on you, just as my Father has conferred on me, a kingdom.' (Luke 22.28–29)

Thought to be the 'Nathanael' whom Philip brought to Jesus, and who was disparaging in his view of Nazareth's inhabitants, Bartholomew became one of the Twelve. Jesus praised his honesty, if not his forthrightness; and Bartholomew, according to tradition, went on to preach in India, eventually being beheaded in Armenia.

Perhaps we also can recall the time when a friend led us to Jesus. If that friend is still alive, can we, on Bartholomew's day, make contact, and say 'Thank You' once again? Or say a prayer if such a meeting is not possible? And can we resolve, in our turn, to bring as many people as we can to Christ? Some may accept him, others may reject him, but we shall have done what we could.

Lives of great men all remind us,
We can make our lives sublime,
And departing leave behind us
Footprints on the sands of time.

(H. W. Longfellow)

❖ The Beheading of John the Baptist 29 August

Jer. 1.4–10; Ps. 11; Heb. 11.32—12.2; Matt. 14.1–12

CLOUD OF WITNESSES

From the epistle: 'Therefore, since we are surrounded by so great a cloud of witnesses, let us also lay aside every weight and the sin that clings so closely, and let us run with perseverance the race that is set before us, looking to Jesus.' (Heb. 12.1–2a)

Who are these witnesses? Those who, even before Jesus came, were tortured, mocked, flogged, imprisoned, stoned, cut in pieces, pierced, tormented, exiled . . . and then the Christians provided yet more martyrs for God's kingdom.

John had had respect, of a sort, from Herod Antipas, tetrarch of Galilee, who knew him to be a good man. But Herodias, Herod's niece and also his brother Philip's wife, and whom Herod himself had later married, was determined to have John eliminated because he (rightly) denounced her marriage as illegal (Matt. 14.4).

While it is honest to fulfil a vow, it is morally wrong if the fulfilling of it means committing a crime. Herod, on the night of John's execution, had no right to make a vow to Herodias' daughter which gave her an opening to ask for John's life. But once the vow had been made, the tetrarch did not have the courage to retract it.

Yet John had completed his mission. He could not have done more with the opportunities God had given him. He had finished his course, and his time had come. God chose such a stormy ministry to end on an equally startling note. We will remember John.

❖ Holy Cross Day 14 September

Num. 21.4–9; Ps. 22.23–28; Phil. 2.6–11; John 3.13–17

POINT OF DEATH

From the epistle: '[Jesus] humbled himself and became obedient to the point of death – even death on a cross.' (Phil. 2.8)

The psalmist describes this humbling in painful detail. While we can only guess at the radiance of glory that Jesus left for thirty-odd years, we are not spared the horrors of what he suffered on the cross. Yet even these are only the physical agonies: much greater was the world's sin, which was the reason for his suffering.

The Emperor Constantine's mother, Helena, is said to have discovered the actual cross of Jesus, in Jerusalem, in the fourth century, though the writers of this event were at pains to emphasize that it was not the wood that was venerated, but the Sacrifice that had hung on it.

Who can tell if faith is really deepened by such a relic; or, indeed, what at some future date an authentication of the Turin Shroud would do for people's faith? Our author of Hebrews says simply: 'Faith is the assurance of things hoped for, the conviction of things not seen' (Heb. 11.1). We can reflect on Calvary today where the cross stands bare – for the sacrifice *has been* made, the Saviour's blood *has been* shed, we *have been* redeemed, our ransom *has been* paid.

❖ **Matthew** 21 September

Prov. 3.13–18; Ps. 119.65–72; 2 Cor. 4.1–6; Matt. 9.9–13

WE DO NOT LOSE HEART

From the epistle: 'Therefore, since it is by God's mercy that we are engaged in this ministry, we do not lose heart.' (2 Cor. 4.1)

Matthew – if the ex-tax collector is the evangelist whom we honour today – knew what it was to receive God's mercy in the call to ministry. From serving a pagan power, and dealing exclusively in the world's currency, Matthew accepted the call of Christ to serve God, and to deal in a divine currency that brought eternal life: the blood of Calvary. He is thought to have himself suffered martyrdom in Ethiopia.

Matthew did not lose heart: his is the second longest Gospel (though divided into more chapters, by a later generation, than Luke's); and he wrote primarily for Jews, although it is Matthew who tells of the non-Jewish Magi, early visitors to the young Jesus.

Perhaps God is telling us to leave a secure profession, to give him our whole attention. He does not pay a monthly salary, but sees to our daily needs; his contract includes no pension scheme, for in eternity no one grows old. He does not tie us to an office desk from nine till five;

instead, he says: 'Take the good news of my gospel to every person on this earth.'

Dare we take up such a challenging engagement?

❖ Michael and All Angels   29 September

Gen. 28.10–17; Ps. 103.19–22; Rev. 12.7–12 or Heb. 1.5–14; John 1.47–51

IN DIVINE SERVICE

From the epistle: 'Are not all angels spirits in the divine service, sent to serve for the sake of those who are to inherit salvation?' (Heb. 1.14)

In the New Testament, Archangel Michael is seen contending with the devil for the body of Moses (Jude 9), and fighting in a heavenly war that sees Satan and his angels exiled to earth (Rev. 12.7ff.). Earlier, in Daniel (10.13, 21; 12.10), he has been guarding the Israelites against Persian and Greek influences.

The great leader of the vast heavenly forces, Michael is the arch-protector of Christians from the devil, who continues to prowl the earth as a lion hunting for prey. His name means 'who is like God'. We can assume that he is very close to God in his ministry, which is as a messenger of might for the truth.

Today, as we focus on Michael and the angelic host, can we glimpse the magnificent unfairness of God, who sets an overwhelmingly large force on our side to help us meet whatever the devil can set against us? We can, with justification, echo the words of Elisha: 'Do not be afraid, for there are more with us than there are with them' (2 Kings 6.16).

Michael Archangel's day has been 29 September since the fifth century, when celebrations in his honour began on the evening preceding his church's dedication in Rome on 30 September.

❖ Luke   18 October

Isa. 35.3–6 or Acts 16.6–12a; Ps. 147.1–7; 2 Tim. 4.5–17; Luke 10.1–9

ONLY LUKE

From the epistle: 'Do your best to come to me soon, for Demas, in love with this present world, has deserted me and gone to Thessalonica;

Crescens has gone to Galatia, Titus to Dalmatia. Only Luke is with me.' (2 Tim. 4.9–11a)

It is recognized that a mission-team on occasion needs to separate and diversify if evangelism is to continue to expand. Paul could hardly have expected to keep everyone together in Rome with him indefinitely, but there is an underlying regret in these verses that all but one have left him (and perhaps for less than cogent reasons) – and a real appreciation of Luke's loyalty.

Luke – doctor, artist, missionary and friend – wrote the third Gospel and Acts. A non-Jew, he was intrigued by Jesus' attitude to Gentiles, and in particular to women, who at that time had a low profile in most of society. Luke is concerned for the under-privileged and under-valued; and his writings are enhanced by the support given to his many references to people and places by many contemporary religious and secular writers.

Whether or not we share in the intellectual talents of Luke, can we reflect today on how our lives demonstrate his even greater virtue of friendship and loyalty?

❖ **Simon and Jude**   28 October

Isa. 28.14–16; Ps. 119.89–96; Eph. 2.19–22; John 15.17–27

THE LORD'S TEMPLE

From the epistle: 'So then you are no longer strangers and aliens, but you are ... a holy temple in the Lord ... built together spiritually into a dwelling place for God.' (Eph. 2.19a, 21b–22)

Simon the Canaanite Zealot, and Jude the author of the New Testament's shortest letter and possibly a relative of Jesus and the brother of James: two members of the elite Twelve, yet these disciples are virtually unknown. What did they do after Pentecost, and where did they preach? Some traditions say they both suffered martyrdom in Persia, though others say that Simon died 'full of years' in Edessa.

For every Christian whose mission makes world news, there are millions whose fame goes with them to the grave: patient workers, loyally serving in small communities, with talents used humbly and generously for a handful of souls.

The Bible says simply that the angels rejoice over every soul saved. God does not differentiate between rich and poor, famous or unknown. He takes no account of mere longevity or brevity of service. It is quality that counts.

Let us stop trying to evaluate our worth. It belongs to God, anyway. We are all stones – every one a vital part – of the Lord's temple.

❖ **Commemoration of the Faithful Departed**   2 November
(All Souls' Day)

Lam. 3.17–26, 31–33 or Wisd. 3.1–9; Ps. 23 or 27.1–6, 16–17; Rom. 5.5–11 or 1 Pet. 1.3–9; John 5.19–25 or 6.37–40

ALL MAY HAVE LIFE

From the gospel: 'This is indeed the will of my Father, that all who see the Son and believe in him may have eternal life; and I will raise them up on the last day.' (John 6.40)

'Be faithful until death, and I will give you the crown of life' (Rev. 2.10c). The condition is simple, the promise is sure. However much we grieve over our departed ones, if they have been faithful to Jesus, they will live in glory for ever. They may have been granted a long life here, or taken quickly. They may – like the penitent thief at Calvary – have had a death-bed conversion, or they may have made Christian headlines. Jesus will raise them all on the last day.

When we sense our loved ones are still, in some indefinable way, with us – they are. When we feel their love – we do. When we remember them as they were – they still are, in our hearts. God in his mercy does not cut off memory when he takes a friend. They no longer have the bodies we recognized, but they are still the people we knew.

Our mind's eye may ache with the strain of trying to pierce the veil between life and death, but Jesus is saying: 'Look at ME. See the faithful departed in Me.'

He is always here (Matt. 28.20) – and so, in him, are they.

❖ Andrew   30 November

Isa. 52.7–10; Ps. 19.1–6; Rom. 10.12–18; Matt. 4.18–22

GREAT FAITH

From the epistle: 'Not all have obeyed the good news; for Isaiah says, "Lord, who has believed our message?" So faith comes from what is heard, and what is heard comes through the word of Christ.' (Rom. 10.16–17)

Andrew had faith when Jesus called: not only to answer the call, but also to fetch Peter to Jesus – and think what that introduction led to! Then, at the miraculous feeding, Andrew had faith that Jesus could do wonders with the schoolboy's lunch that he brought to his Master.

Faith in the unknown and unseen takes one right into the risk business; but when it is based on the word of Christ, the risk has already been taken – by a God who deals in the impossible, who knows the unknown, and who can see what to us is invisible. It is as though each morning we launch out into the deep end of the day's ocean, knowing that because we have the talent to swim, our feet do not need to touch the bottom. We have the word of Christ: we do not need to see the future, or to fear the unknown. Jesus tells us: 'Follow me.' Just follow. Leave everything – leave your fears, your inhibitions, your caveats and conditions.

Simply follow, in faith.

❖ Stephen   26 December

2 Chron. 24.20–22; Ps. 119.161–168; Acts 7.51–60 or Gal. 2.16b–20; Matt. 23.34–39

A GODLY WAITER

From the Acts: 'You stiff-necked people, uncircumcised in heart and ears, you are forever opposing the Holy Spirit, just as your ancestors used to do.' (Acts 7.51)

This is a waiter talking! Does it shock you that someone can break so far out of the mould? But Stephen was a waiter who was also 'full of grace and power', who had done 'great wonders and signs' (Acts 6.8). God has no neat pigeonholes for jobs and classes such as we have: a shepherd called Caedmon could compose beautiful songs; a parlourmaid called Gladys Aylward rescued a hundred Chinese children from certain death, and evangelized many more; and a waiter called Stephen preached the sermon of his life to become the first Christian martyr.

If we could see ourselves as God sees us, we might well discard what presently seems essential, and also realize gifts that we did not know we had. Like Stephen, should we be called in the Church to what may appear a lowly work, let us bring to it everything we possess.

It may not lead to martyrdom – but it will certainly take us nearer to eternal life . . . which will be shared with Stephen the one-time waiter.

❖ John   27 December

Exod. 33.7–11a; Ps. 117; 1 John 1; John 21.19b–25

GOD IS LIGHT

From the epistle: 'This is the message we have heard from him and proclaim to you, that God is light and in him there is no darkness at all.' (1 John 1.5)

Did one man write all the 'Johannine' material in the New Testament? It is unlikely, but the material itself is more important than the identity of the author(s). The 'John' who wrote Revelation was exiled to Patmos 'because of the word of God and the testimony of Jesus' (Rev. 1.9); and the author of the fourth Gospel identifies the word with Jesus (John 1.1f.), while the writer of 1 John sees the same message as bringing God's light to us (cf. John 1.4f.).

When Joshua had the Israelites on the border of the Promised Land, he was prepared to lead them in to possess it. But some were afraid, some argued, some just wanted to stay where they were. Similarly, people rejected, or feared, or argued about the light that Jesus brought. John, reviewing the ministry of Jesus, marvels that so much could be offered, yet so little accepted. God had been at such pains to give people a chance – and most of them were passing up the opportunity.

Has God knocked at your heart with a vision, a revelation, a suggestion, a command? (Rev. 3.20.) He is a Gentleman; he will not enter until we have opened the door from our side. How long do we plan to keep him waiting?

❖ Holy Innocents

Jer. 31.15–17; Ps. 124; 1 Cor. 1.26–29; Matt. 2.8–13

THE WEAK ARE CHOSEN

From the epistle: 'God chose what is foolish in the world to shame the wise; God chose what is weak in the world to shame the strong.' (1 Cor. 1.27)

Can we hear the cries of these little children in the razzmatazz of the modern Christmas? We wonder why the carnage had to be: why faith should be tested; we puzzle at a God who could allow innocent children to be sacrificed on such a scale. Could not Jesus have saved the world without this anguish?

Of course he could. But God does not intend anyone's faith to come cheaply. At every point, he makes the step of faith count: for Jesus and for us. The resurrection could have shaken the whole earth on its axis – but where would faith have been if everyone had been given no choice but to believe?

The children of Bethlehem may have expected to live normal lives: instead, they were taken early to a glorious life. Jesus looked like any Jewish child – but after 30 years of convention, he would accomplish in three short years the destruction of eternal death, and would found a Church to outlive time itself. He would change normal people into world-changers; and he would restore hope to a world that had lost its direction.

God's energies are never wasted – or he would never have chosen us for his service, would he?

Biblical text Index

9.16 25
10.13 42
11.23–24 74
11.25b–26 50
12.2, 8 19
13.11 22
2 Cor. 1.21–22 29
4.1 34, 151
4.5 33, 75
4.16–17 77
5.14a, 16a 145
6.11–13 81
8.9 83
12.7b–9a 86
Gal. 1.1, 10 76
1.11–12 136
2.16a, 19b–20a 80
3.28 82
4.4–5 148
4.6 12
Eph. 1.8b–9 87
1.8–10 140
2.12 90
2.19 123
2.19a, 21b–22 153
3.6 15
3.18–19 92
4.11–12 139

4.11–13a 94
4.26–27 96
5.18c–19 98
6.14–17 100
Phil. 2.8 150
2.12b–13 109
3.10 45
3.20–21 40
Col. 1.9–10 88
1.18 31
1 Thess. 1.8a 115
2.2 117
3.9 2
5.11 130
5.16–18 5
2 Thess. 3.8–9 132
1 Tim. 2.1–2 109
2 Tim. 1.11–12 113
2.8 136
3.16–17 120
4.9–11a 153
4.17 143
Titus 1.4a 136
3.4–5 10
Heb. 1.3a 112
1.14 152
2.17 23
2.18 11

4.15 114
5.5b, 6b 116
9.13–14 127
12.1–2a 150
12.1b–2a 99
12.28–29 101
13.5–6 103
Jas. 1.22 102
2.15–17 104
3.2 106
1 Pet. 1.17 147
1.23 58
2.4–5 62, 122
2.24 60
3.13–14a, 15 64
4.1–2 51
2 Pet. 1.20–21 33
3.9 3
1 John 1.5 156
2.1b–2 57
3.4a, 7 59
5.10 68
Rev. 4.1 32
5.9–10 18
5.11–12 60
7.9 124
19.6b, 7 20
21.1–2 124

Subject Index